SHADOW
--- OF ---
WHISKEY VALLEY

By
ERMAN SANDS

Shadows of Whiskey Valley

Copyright © 2017 by Erman Sands

All rights reserved.

No part of this publication may be reproduced, distributed, or transmitted in any form or by any means, including photocopying, recording, or other electronic or mechanical methods, without the prior written permission of the publisher, except in the case of brief quotations embodied in critical reviews and certain other noncommercial uses permitted by copyright law.

ISBN-13: 978-1984041807

ISBN-10: 1984041800

Contents

DEDICATION IV
CHAPTER 1 1
CHAPTER 2 26
CHAPTER 3 48
CHAPTER 4 68
CHAPTER 5 88
CHAPTER 6 111
CHAPTER 7 139
CHAPTER 8 147
CHAPTER 9 164
CHAPTER 10 184
CHAPTER 11 203
CHAPTER 12 219
CHAPTER 13 236
CHAPTER 14 256
CHAPTER 15 274
CHAPTER 16 282

DEDICATION

This book is dedicated to my wife, a loving family and friends both near and far, who give unbelievable support to my writing efforts.

CHAPTER 1

The rock skipped three, four, five times across the clear water before it sank. Dave spun with a big grin and flashed a thumbs up victory salute. Vera Lee sat beside the picnic basket with a smile. Boys were so immature.

Rearranging her skirts on the blanket Vera Lee waited patiently. The warm spring sun felt good on her bare arms. Something was bothering Dave. She knew him well enough to wait until he worked his thoughts out and brought them up. Was he mulling a wedding date? Leaning back she allowed the sun to warm her.

"Three days to graduation," Dave flopped onto

the edge of the blanket and picked a blade of grass. "I have a job driving a log truck for the summer." He toyed with the blade of grass. "I also have another bit of news. I've been accepted into the Internal Revenue Service Academy."

"You've been what, where?" Vera Lee lost her smile. She sat bolt upright. Cold fingers closed around her heart.

"I have passed the entire test and other requirements to get into the enforcement branch of the Internal Revenue Service. I start next September." Dave spoke soberly, softly and then placed the end of the grass blade in his mouth and waited for Vera Lee's reaction.

"I thought we'd discussed all this silly revenue agent stuff and decided we wouldn't to do it. If you become a revenue agent everyone in the valley will hate you and you'll have to leave the valley." Vera Lee became more agitated by the moment. She leaped to her feet and placing both hands on her hips she faced Dave.

Dave spit the blade of grass out of his mouth. "I

plan to leave the valley. I could never serve among kinfolk and friends. Outside of you, I have nothing but memories left in this valley."

Removing her hands from her hips Vera lee wrung them. "We discussed this and you said … "

"I said I would think about it. I have thought about it. You know this has been my dream for a long time. This is a once in a lifetime chance. If I pass this one up I'll never get another. There is no way I'm going to stay here and dirt farm, run a chain saw or bootleg whiskey!" Dave vowed leaping to his feet.

Vera Lee sucked in a sharp breath. Her eyes grew hard and her lips stretched thin. "This valley is my home. Mom and Dad are here. I have no plans to leave or be shunned. You can forget this silly revenue agent notion."

Vera Lee had always been the little princess flitting from one idea to another like a butterfly, taking nothing seriously. A strong capable father, doting mother and dating the most popular boy from childhood brought Vera Lee to be the Queen

Bee of her age set in the valley.

If she married Dave and he became a revenue agent he would be shunned and hated, so would she, and leave this valley? No way! Her parents lived in this valley. If she moved her social position would be gone. She planned to live, die and be buried in this valley.

Dave was quiet but determined. Fiddling with the grass blade he let the moments slip by. He turned his face into the cool breeze that came rippling over the water. His eyes drifted to the white water boiling over the rocks into a still pool. A beaver's tail slapped a warning to his clan. The intruders are still here. In the past weeks Dave spent many sleepless nights wrestling with this problem. He fought this battle and came to his conclusions.

His high marks on the written tests and his athletic abilities on the physical test earned him a once in a lifetime chance to get into the academy. Less than five percent of the qualified applicants were accepted. "Come September I go to the academy," he said quietly but firmly.

Vera Lee stamped her foot and screamed, "Go! I will not go with you. I will not marry a stinking revenue agent. When you get over this silly notion let me know. I will be waiting." Vera Lee grabbed the picnic basket in one hand and the blanket in the other. "I will be waiting." She repeated on her way out.

During the three days to graduation Dave maintained an icy silence. Vera Lee kept asking herself, "Am I right?" She was sure Dave would come to her point of view. This state of affairs rolled through the summer months into Dave's departure date.

The big Greyhound bus was rumbling into the station when a tearful Vera Lee arrived. "Dave won't you reconsider?"

"Not likely, I will be back when I graduate. Perhaps you will change your mind by then. As you have said, I will be waiting." Dave struggled for the strength to climb the steps.

The driver popped the air brakes twice and glared at Dave. He had seen many sad farewells. Hesitating on the second step Dave said, "I'll be back when I ..." The big air driven doors slammed in Dave's face.

Vera Lee watched the bus disappear in the distance. *He will come to his senses and come home to me,* she promised herself.

Later that day Jason dropped into Harper's store.

"I hear Dave left for the Academy today," Mr. Harper moved down the counter gathering the supplies Jason ordered.

"Yeah," Jason's answer was short and curt.

"I tell you Jason," Mr. Harper shook his head as he sat the last of Jason's order in a box. "I thought the fight was on. Dave was here in the store when Pots and the Swann brothers came in. Pots was carrying a jug and he offered Dave a drink. Dave looked Pots in eye, smiled, and said real politely, but hard and firm like, "No, thank you."

"Dave looked like his Grandpa standing there. He had a smile on his lips but those eyes were as hard as granite. There wasn't one grain of give in him.

"Old Pots swelled and bristled but he thought better of it. He and the Swann brothers walked out the door tossing revenuer cracks between themselves."

"I can't figure that boy out. I'm glad my daughter saw through him in time." Jason Marley picked up the box and walked out the door. Dave Miloy was not his favorite topic of conversation right now.

Time dragged on. Vera Lee was lonely but held firmly to her convictions.

The winter blew itself out. Two summers had came and gone. The red leaves of the Black Gum contrasted with the yellows of the forest. Waiting for the winter winds the forest was somber and quiet.

A fall breeze rustled and rattled its way through the crisp frost bitten leaves to spread the message, winter is coming.

A fox squirrel dropped his acorn and raced to the top an old oak tree. He settled on the limb in front of the hole he called home and scolded Vera Lee vigorously for interrupting his food gathering efforts.

Standing on the creek bank, the scene of her last picnic with Dave, Vera Lee neither saw nor heard any of the beauty around her. Seizing a stone she angrily flung it into the water. It did not skip like Dave's stone had; it sank like a heavy heart. The same old beaver sent a warning slap echoing down the creek.

Drawing Dave's letters from her pocket Vera Lee reread them. She was so lonely. She searched for clues to a weakening of Dave's resolve to finish the academy training. There were none. The last letter had a vague restless feeling about it. Could this restlessness be a sign of Dave's resolve weakening? Or, could it be a weakening of his affection for her? Had he found someone else?

It was a heart rending situation. Her instincts and loneliness told her to fly to Dave but the cold calculating side of her brain told her to hold out and she would get all her wishes fulfilled. An apologetic Dave would be back.

At breakfast Jason chewed his bacon and eggs and watched his daughter toy with the food on her plate. "You've made the right decision." Jason informed Vera Lee. "That boy is no good. Turning on his people this way, he will be contacting you soon trying to wiggle his way back in. I hope you're smart enough to say no."

Vera Lee's heart jumped. Jason's warning had the opposite effect Jason was trying for. Jason thought Dave was coming to her! That is just what she was wanted. That is what she was hoping and praying for!

Taking the letters from her pocket Vera Lee reread them. She had not answered Dave's letters but she kept them close. The letters were thumb marked and wrinkled from being read so often.

Grabbing a rock she angrily flung it at the beaver then hung her head and cried.

Two weeks later word came through the wind. Dave is coming back to the valley! The backwoods telegraph reached Vera Lee. There are no telephones, no telegraphs; it is amazing how fast news of a happening spreads from one end of the valley to the other.

Most folks were furious. They thought Dave was returning to harass people with whiskey stills. Vera Lee knew better. Dave's return to the valley was linked to his desire to see her.

On that faithful day beside the swimming hole Dave told her he was leaving the valley. He was not ever going to serve among his people.

He was coming for her. He would contact her soon. She had won it all.

The communities' reaction to Dave's return as a revenue lawman was exactly as she had predicted. They were furious. Even the Sunday go to meeting church people who believed running a whiskey still was a sin were mad at Dave.

Dave would come to his senses and toss that badge as soon as he realized the full cost of wearing it. The long lonely months of waiting suddenly became worth the trouble.

Vera Lee sat in front of the mirror arranging and rearranging her hair. She thought better messing with her hair and she had some heavy planning to do. The annual pie supper that provided the small amount of money needed for cemetery maintenance was coming up soon.

She was sure Dave would attend the pie supper. She felt sorry for him. He was an outgoing type of guy and he was going to be so put out when no one spoke to him. She kept an ear open to the road into her house. There were no other dwellings on this road. If she heard an engine she knew it was coming to her house. She was positive he was coming. He would be here. Hat in hand, he would be here.

She heard it. She was sure she heard an engine slowing for the creek crossing in front of the house. Vera Lee flew to the window of her upstairs bedroom. Pulling the curtain back she saw Dave leap from the cab and drop down to pet Jason's decrepit old hound dog. Dave was back! Dave was back!

Before Vera Lee could force her legs to bolt for the stairway Jason came stalking around the corner. Jason moved with a measured tread. His hands were on his hips. She had learned long ago the futility of arguing with him when he tipped and set his head in this manner.

Murmuring angry words floated up to her window. When Dave stood the light reflections from the badge pinned to his shirt flashed through her window. This struck her like a physical blow. Dave slammed the door on his pickup and made a spinning gravel throwing turn toward the creek. Gravel pinged off the porch swing she and Dave used to sit on.

Vera Lee slowly backed to her bed and sat down. "There will be other times and places," she promised herself. "The pie supper is coming up. I'll see him there.

Vera Lee carefully prepared her box for the cemetery pie supper. No one was supposed know who prepared the box when it went up for auction but every year she put a yellow rose on the box somewhere. Dave knew which box to buy.

This time she crafted a big beautiful yellow rose from crepe paper, surrounded it with a yellow ribbon accent, and then taped it on the center of her box. This was sure to catch Dave's attention.

She had no intention of eating with Dave when

he bought her box but it would give her a chance to talk to him. It would also give him a chance to apologize and beg for forgiveness.

Ever alert for Dave's arrival Vera Lee maintained a presence near the door. When he did come, she was very aware of his arrival. To her horror, Dave wandered around the parking lot looking in the windows of the parked cars. She knew several of the people present always brought a jar of whiskey with them. It was a tradition.

Was Dave going to make arrests at the biggest social function of the year? The burnished star on his shirt reflected a flash of light. Her blood boiled. Her face flushed red. How could Dave be so stubbornly stupid?

When Dave pushed through the door she glared at him. Slowly her nose rose and she regally marched across the room and engaged the boy who lived next door in conversation. She kept an eye on Dave.

A look of consternation washed over Dave's face. He stood dumbfounded. Vera Lee was pleased. It served him right! Let him stand and stew in his juice. At best everyone would ignore him. At worst someone would challenge him.

Lesa, the local school teacher, broke with the group of people she was conversing with and approached Dave. Vera Lee couldn't understand the words but Lesa was smiling from ear to ear. Hooking a possessive hand through Dave's arm Lesa dragged him to the group she'd been engaged with.

Vera Lee's anger knew no bounds. *How could this brazen hussy approach my man?* She asked herself.

Mr. Harper tapped on the portable mic borrowed from a local musician for the pie supper auction. "Ladies and Gentlemen," he roared. "The pie supper auction is about to begin!"

There was the usual joshing and laughing as Mr. Harper worked his way through the pies until he came to the one with a big yellow rose on top of it.

Mr., Harper held the box at several different angles looking at the yellow rose. "Folks this rose alone ought to be worth five dollars." Hefting the weight of the box Mr. Harper held it high. "I can guarantee there is a full meal in here and it smells good. I smell fried chicken. What am I bid?"

There was a hesitation and a one dollar bid came from the boy next door. Dave smiled and turned his back.

Vera Lee's cheeks burned red then white. *He did not bid on my box. Not one bid!* Vera Lee thought. She staggered to a bench near the wall and sat down. With a mighty effort she fought the tears back. There was no way she was going to let Dave see her cry!

The rest of the evening was a blur. Dave bid an outrageous amount on that mousy school teacher's box. Then Dave and Pots fought. Vera Lee hoped Pots would kill Dave but it was not to be. Even though Pots pulled a knife Dave rapidly and soundly whipped Pots. After the fight Dave departed.

Vera Lee rose intending to accompany Dave to his car and tell him how sorry she was but that school teaching hussy slipped her hand through the space behind Dave's arm and escorted him out.

Vera Lee walked to the window and watched

an animated conversation between Lesa and Dave before he drove off. *I have been wrong* Vera Lee told herself. *I have been so wrong. What can I do to correct that?*

None of Vera Lee's plans to accidentally meet Dave and explain things bore any fruit. He was as elusive as a doe with a new fawn. He was either gone or quickly disappeared from any place she went.

Rumors floated up and down the valley about his growing infatuation with Lesa Turner. Vera Lee hated Lesa. That hussy was stealing her Man!

Then the awful day came when Dave informed her Jason Marley had been arrested in Kansas while delivering a load of whiskey. On this day Vera Lee hated Dave and everyone else in this world. She went into seclusion, never leaving the farmstead until the day of Jason's trial.

The Judge flowed into the courtroom and climbed behind the highly polished desk. Looking around the courtroom he smiled. He was God of all he surveyed.

Vera Lee seated herself on the front row. She

wanted to be as near to her father as possible.

Jason Marley entered the courtroom escorted by a burly Deputy Sheriff at each elbow and one following. He had not been a model prisoner.

It was his face that shocked Vera Lee. He'd aged ten years since being incarcerated.

The rest of the trial was a blur. The lawyers traded jabs and the trial droned on. The outcome was a foregone conclusion.

The sanctimonious Judge made a few remarks about the bootleggers ruining the moral fiber of the nation and disobeying the law. After his speech he asked Jason if he had anything to say before he passed sentence on him.

"Judge," Jason rose slowly from the defense table. The three Deputies braced themselves. "Don't try to lecture me on what is right and what is wrong." Jason raised both hands. The Deputies shifted their feet. "See the calluses on these hands judge. They were earned by honest work feeding and caring for my family. Every year they produce things other folks need to eat, drink and be happy. They have paid taxes and maintained things. These hands have grown rough in the service of the human race.

"Now look at your hands Judge. They're as soft as a baby's hands. Those are the hands of a thief. They produce nothing to advance the human race. They live by stealing the things produced by the labors of other people.

"You will take a couple jugs of this whiskey you are about to sentence me for making and you will have drunken parties. While this is going on you will make foul mouthed remarks about me rotting in your stinking prison for making it.

"I know the District Attorney will need a couple jugs. Look at that nose. Anyone can tell he's been an alcoholic for years. When prohibition was in full swing he still obtained his alcohol. Who knows, I might be partly guilty for him being an alcoholic. I'm sure he drank whiskey I made at one time or another.

"The Sheriff will manage to sell a few jars before what little that's left gets destroyed. The money I paid him to leave my still alone seems to have been wasted.

"I have no doubt Judge, if I'd been able to walk in here with a fist full of dollars, I'd be on my way home now, a free man."

The judge listened patiently until Jason ran out of words and wind. "Mr. Marley," the Judge shifted a handful of paperwork on his desk. "You have said some unjust, unfounded and unfair things about the officers of this court. It is plain you have no remorse for the violations you're convicted of. I therefore sentence you to the maximum sentence, Fifteen years in the Federal Correctional Center at El Reno, Oklahoma."

The Judge whacked the gavel and stalked out of the court room.

After a tearful parting with Jason, Ruth and Vera Lee returned home to a seemingly empty house and deserted farm.

Vera Lee rubbed her temples. So much to learn and so little time to learn it in, she hired Pots' older sons to help with the farm work.

Mother shrank into herself. She spent hours

conversing with her needle. Mother was able to tend house and cook but her vacant stare at the dinner table was almost more than Vera Lee could bear.

Vera Lee had suddenly been thrust from a spoiled, pampered little princess into the role of farm manager, farm labor and head of household. She'd always been the little princess flitting from one idea to another like a butterfly, taking nothing seriously. With a strong capable father, doting mother and dating the most popular boy in school brought Vera Lee to be the queen bee of her age set in the valley.

Now, she'd lost both the men in her life. She'd been left alone to determine what crops to plant, when to plant them and required to put in the long grueling hours of labor required to grow them. The hot sun drew gallons of sweat and tanned her skin to a dark brown.

The blood of the frontier Marley's flowed in her veins. The harder the going got the more determined she became. Like her father, when she set her sights on something nothing could bend her judgment. Her hair was a fright and her hands became the calloused hands of a hard working man.

Vera Lee's social life disappeared. There was no time for it. Since that hateful hussy of a school teacher stole Dave from her she was ashamed to show her face in public. Most of her time was spent in the fields. She was there when the sun rose and was still there when the sun set.

She spent eighteen hours hoeing corn on Lesa and Dave's wedding day. She could not, would not, accept any responsibility for the breakup between herself and Dave. Every weed she chopped had Lesa's face on it.

Idly ruffling the pages of the ledger book Vera Lee sat in deep thought, *I must do something. I've lost money the past two years in a row. Daddy was a good manager he made a lot of money. If he had not squirreled it away and left mother and I a good nest egg we'd be in dire straights now.*

I suppose we could sell the place and leave the valley. We have enough money at the present time to relocate us in the city. Perhaps I could find work there. Vera Lee yanked the brush through a tangle in her hair. *I will not leave this valley!* She vowed. *I suppose I could put in a hog house and sell pigs.*

Daddy did well. He got a lot the money he made from the whiskey he peddled up north. Vera's face flushed, "*I used to call him stingy but he was looking forward to these days. He amassed more money than anyone expected. I must do something. I couldn't face daddy if I spend all his money while he is gone.* Vera Lee slowly drew the brush through her hair.

I have daddy's still. I could make whiskey. I might get some of daddy's Customers that Dave's Revenuers haven't caught. The idea shocked Vera Lee. Her shoulders rose and she sat upright to think about it.

Dave! What would Dave think if he caught me making whiskey? Everybody in the country thinks Dave knew Lesa was driving the Ford delivering bootleg whiskey. He married her anyway.

The old days of smoky fire boxes and fire breathing automobiles is over, there must be a better way. Vera Lee continued to brush her hair and mused, *Deception and brains will have to replace brawn and speed.*

Taking up a legal pad she wrote headers for four columns.

SUPPLIES FOR MAKING DISTILLING TRANSPORTING SELLING

After thinking about it for awhile she added a fifth column. PEOPLE I CAN HIRE AND TRUST.

Before she progressed farther into her plans she drove up for a conversation with Pots' widow. Pots' sons had worked on the farm for the past two years. Better than two years, one reached legal age and the other will have by the time she put a plan together and worked it out. Still, she wanted their mom's blessing before she involved them in an illegal whiskey making operation.

Wheeling around the corner she studied the house the people of the community built for Pots' widow after his untimely demise. The community held a pie supper to raise the funds needed for material and everyone pitched in on the labor. A new house rose on the ashes of the old. The new house wasn't as large or as fancy as the one the Swan brothers burned but it was a roof over their heads until the boys earned enough to build better.

Vera Lee admired the miniature whiskey still the boys had built. She took a small glass of whiskey from it and settled in the swing on the shady side of the front porch. She took a sip from the small snuff glass.

"Cricket, this is excellent whiskey." She took another sip and waited.

"It should be. The boys had the best teacher who ever ran a still."

"That brings me to the purpose of this visit. I'm going to make some shine and I want the best to make it. I want to market the best whiskey ever made. I know the boys are full grown young men or soon will be but I want your blessing before I approach them.

"If you disapprove I will look elsewhere." Vera Lee settled back to let Cricket think.

"We sure could use the money. Where and how will they make the whiskey? Dave Maloy has sure made it hard on anyone making whiskey in this country." Cricket knew the full story of Vera Lee's involvement with Dave. Was it possible that Dave would allow Vera Lee to make and sell whiskey?

"I can't answer any questions. The more information out the more likely your sons are to be caught if they go in with me." Vera Lee sat the snuff glass on the porch rail, walked across to the steps and hesitated. She watched the birds flitting in the treetops and smelled the breeze flowing through the lilac bushes. "They did catch Pots," she said softly. "And he was the best."

"They did not catch Pots!" Cricket denied violently. "He was betrayed by his friends. Low down sorry friends he supported and trusted for years." Cricket lowered her face into her hands and sobbed.

Vera Lee retraced her steps across the porch and hugged Cricket.

"Take care of my babies," Cricket sobbed.

"I will, "Vera Lee promised. "I will do the best I can." She repeated and she meant it.

CHAPTER 2

A cool wind blew odd pieces of paper, leaves, and other debris across the prison parking lot. Vera Lee wheeled the red Chevrolet pickup into a parking space. Placing the transmission in the lowest gear she set the parking brake. Letting out a big sigh she laid her head on the steering wheel. This part of the growing plan she liked least of all. She was crossing the Rubicon. There would no turning back after this visit.

What was Daddy going to say?

Vera Lee had not informed mother she was going to the prison today. Hurrying across the lot she was shown into a small visiting room on the first floor.

Being convicted of a non-violent crime Jason was permitted to visit at a table with no glass divider between him and Vera Lee. There were, however, four cameras and a microphone recording the visit. A guard was also stationed close enough to hear their conversation.

Vera Lee was very familiar with her dad's temper and out bursts. She needed him to stay cool calm and collected today. They must speak in a playful code they had developed during her childhood. The code began when she was a small child. Jason would wiggle his fingers to tell her to quite down. Later he expanded it to 'sit down'. Vera Lee expanded the language by begging him to let her run and play with the rest of the unruly kids. By her teenage years they could carry on a conversation in code and no one was the wiser.

She fervently hoped she could get Jason understanding without arousing the guard's suspicions. She wanted no suspicions started at this point.

The guard ushered Jason in and crossing his

arms leaned against the wall with a bored look on his face. This was not his favorite assignment.

Vera Lee watched her father's face, trying to gauge his mood. Jason's stride was strong and he had a smile on his face. The highlight of the month was a visit from his little princess. It hurt him very much that no physical contact was permitted. He longed to sweep her up and swing her around the way he used to. He sent a questioning look at the guard who read his mind and shook his head in a slow negative manner.

"Where is your Mother?" Jason questioned right away.

"She didn't feel up to the trip today." Vera Lee looked hard into Jason's eyes. Her right hand lay on the table. With the fingers pointed straight toward Jason. The hand moved slightly left to right and back, this was a not true signal.

Jason hesitated. His eyes flew to the guard without turning his head. The guard leaned against the wall seemingly wrapped in his thoughts and being bored.

The four cameras relentlessly bore down on them. Jason leaned forward and laid both hands on the table from the elbows forward. The movement drew the guard's attention. He watched closely. Nothing seemed amiss so after a few moments he went back to his daydreams.

Jason and Vera Lee discussed what crops to plant, who she could trust to plant them, when to plant them, how to work them and different possibilities in where to market the produce.

Jason fought hard not to show emotion at first. As the conversation continued he had many emotions and fears he could find no way to express. He began to see his little princess in a new light. Could she have grown this much in two years? Was she ever the scatter brained young lady he'd thought her to be?

My god, he thought looking across the table, *she's the spitting image of my mom at that age. Perhaps my disappointment at her not being a son was premature.*

Pride rose in his breast. That girl is made out the good stuff. She is a Marley!

Jason looked at the cameras again. He had to work hard at keeping his voice even and his movements to a bare minimum. Their skills at the code increased as their memories were brushed up.

Vera Lee was in a much better mood when she left the prison. Her fears that Jason would explode and forbid her to set up a whiskey still had been averted. He'd been against the idea, most especially at first but as time went on she had convinced him she was mature and smart enough to pull it off.

She drove with swarms of possibilities circling her head. Occasionally something slowed and attached itself to the plan forming in her mind.

The big bright full moon hung in the night sky and bright stars twinkled from horizon to horizon when the Chevy slowed and stopped at the gate in the picket fence. Jack hopped painfully to the gate on three legs. Old age stiffened the joints in his body. Vera Lee dropped to her knees and gave Jack a hug that made every nerve in his dilapidated old body tremble.

"I feel great," she declared to the old dog. Rising

she spread her arms and spun in a circle. "For the past two years I've staggered around like a drunk and absorbed blow after blow. No longer world! Vera Lee takes it no longer!" She turned a dancing spin in the other direction.

Jack didn't know what the excitement was about but he knew something good had happened. He raised his head and let out a long mournful howl.

The needle stopped in mid stitch when Vera Lee danced into the room. Mother threw a questioning look at her daughter.

"I'm tired. I'm going to bed mom." Vera Lee hugged mother and breezed out.

"Well needle, it's time something good happened here. That poor girl has had more than her share of trouble." Mother didn't know what the occasion for the light mood was but she'd settle for most anything good at this point.

Mother was fussing with something on the cook stove when Vera Lee slid into her place at the breakfast table. She sat in the same place she sat when she was a small child. The head of the table was always Jason Marley's and would remain empty until he returned from prison.

"You seem to be feeling better." Vera Lee ventured.

"I am, honey. It has been rough with Jason in prison and you moping around working yourself to death." Mother carried food to the table and placed it in front of Vera Lee. "You've perked up the last few days. Have you found a young man? Is it Jeff or Junior Rayett?"

"Mother! They're babies!" Vera Lee blushed.

"No, they are young men who admire you greatly." Mother said firmly.

"I don't know what I would have done without them. but they are two hard working dear friends." Vera Lee agreed with mother's assertion that Jeff and Junior had grown into men.

"Oh dear," Mother picked up one of Vera lee's hands. "Oh dear" she repeated turning the hand to inspect the other side. "They're so rough.

"You should take some time off and go shopping for something that will smooth those hands up."

Mother shook her head.

Vera Lee held her hands in front of her and turned them back and forth. "It's like Daddy told the Judge. These are the hands that are making us a living. They are producing hands." Having said this she looked at her mother. There was more light in her mother's eyes than she had seen in a long time.

"You should do less work and go shopping.' Mother was adamant.

"There has been no time to go to town. There is too much to do. Pots' sons, Jeff and Junior, are hard workers and know more than I do but their knowledge is limited and it takes us more time to complete a job." Vera Lee watched her mother closely. "If there is something you need put it on the list. I'm sending in an order for groceries, some plow shares and a truck load of seed. If there is anything you need add it to the list and they will deliver it.

"You haven't been off the place since Pots and the Swann Brother's funeral." Mother continued.

"I haven't been to Harper's store since then

either. I don't want to bump into Dave or that slut Lesa. People are probably still laughing at me for letting Lesa steal Dave from me." Vera Lee said bitterly.

"But Mom, things are going to change. Jeff and Junior can handle the things Dad did here. I'm going to travel some and later I'm going to build a hog house. We're going to raise and sell pigs. Vera Lee raised her work worn hands and looked at them. "Things will be better," she promised them.

Each day Vera Lee took a walk. While she was walking she was planning. Hours were spent reading newspapers from various states. Her appearance became important to her once more.

She pulled the name and address of a middle man In Nebraska from her pocket. He bought from the whiskey stills and sold to the bootleggers. On the way north she thought about what she was going to say to this middle man. It was time to move on.

"I know you bought moonshine from Jason Marley." Vera lee looked around the used car dealership the middleman used to front for his real business. "Until he got caught anyway, He's in prison and won't be selling anything for awhile."

"Marley always delivered good stuff." The short balding middleman walked around the counter in the used car agency that covered his true occupation. "Will your product be as good as his?" The man asked bluntly.

"Mine will be better. I have better whiskey stills and better operators." Vera Lee's dark eyes bored into the man like a rattler holding a rat spell bound. Cleo, the middleman squirmed. He'd never seen such cold beauty in his life. The lady was beautiful but when he looked deep into those dark eyes his blood seemed to gel.

"When can you deliver? How much can you deliver?" Cleo was interested.

"It will be a little while before I can start delivery. I plan to deliver five hundred gallons a week." Vera Lee waited while the man digested this.

"Five hundred gallons a week!" Cleo was shocked. "I can't handle five hundred gallon a week. I'd have to take in some partners … I .."

"No partners! I deal with one person." Vera Lee rose.

"Now hold on. I didn't mean people you have to deal with. I meant more buyers."

"Think it over I'll be in touch." Vera Lee buzzed out of the office.

The next day, Vera Lee and the President of the Barnes Furniture Manufacturing Plant strolled along the assembly lines. They hesitated here and there to observe one or another phase of furniture making.

"I see you use a lot of oak lumber in your factory Mr. Barnes. I have a lot of oak trees and a log truck to haul them. If you'd give me contracts to set a small sawmill on the vacant lots across the street I could sell the oak lumber to you at least a ten percent cheaper than you are paying now." Vera stopped walking and waited for Barnes answer.

"In the first place call me Don. My father was Mr. Barnes. Wouldn't it be cheaper to saw the timber in Oklahoma and haul the lumber here?"

"Not really, we plan to cut the slabs into firewood.

You know how expensive firewood is up here. We plan to market the sawdust and bark to local gardeners and landscapers so we will sell the sum total of the logs we haul in," Vera Lee justified the hauling of whole logs. "There will never be a big accumulation of anything on the vacant lots."

"Come to my office and we'll discuss it." Barnes was mentally calculating the bottom line of a ten percent saving on lumber.

It was time for the annual pie supper again. Vera Lee had skipped the past two pie suppers but knew she had to join the world of the living if she carried her plans to fruitation. She prepared the same box that brought her so much anguish the last pie supper she attended. She hung her head and cried when she fastened the handcrafted yellow rose to the top of the box.

Mentally, she slapped herself. Her head snapped up into the position she had seen Jason's head set in on so many occasions. Her eyes took on a hard glare. "You will take it no longer," she said, "You're a Marley. You will go in tonight with pride written all over you."

.The sky was a clear blue when she wheeled into the pie supper parking lot. The sun peeked over the lip of the earth and a cool breeze cooled her cheek when she retrieved the box with yellow rose and approached the building. Handing the box to a young lady waiting outside the door she too a deep breath and shoved the door open.

All heads turned when she stepped through the doors into a school room where the annual pie supper was held. It was like the old Vera Lee had been resurrected. Her dress was stunning, her hair professionally done, her skin was radiant and a smile lit up her lips. The black eyes were hard, calculating and missed nothing.

They were even more surprised when she made a special greeting to Dave and Lesa Maloy. Vera Lee made it clear, to one and all; the old mournful days were over. She was back to claim her place in the valley.

Mister Harper was most glad to see her back. Not only had the heads turned at her entrance, several of the country swains slipped him five dollars to point out the box she brought to the pie supper.

Mister Harper began the pie auction with the same jokes and fun poking as usual. The crowd was in a mellow mood and chuckling at each unfortunate person Mister Harper singled out.

When the box with a yellow rose on the lid came to his hand Mister Harper reached into his pocket and pulled out a wad of bills and waved them at the crowd, "This next box has already taken in twenty-five dollars in donations and has not been auctioned off yet." He handed the wad of bills to the secretary. There are several of these young yahoos who wanted to know the person that put together such a pretty box." There was general laughter from the crowd.

"Since there was so much interest in this box I'm going to have to break the rules and tell you this box was prepared by the beautiful young lady conversing with Cricket Rayette. I've been in love with her since the day she was born but she won't give an old geezer like me the time of day.

"Welcome back Miss Vera Lee." A bright crimson

blush slipped up her throat and covered her face. "Now come on boys, open your pocket books and let's see if any of you can do a better job of making a hit with this pretty lady than I have."

Pointing to the first fellow who slipped him five dollars Mister Harper bellowed into the mike, "Did I hear a bid of ten thousand dollars?" The fellow turned white and the crowd roared.

The bidding was spirited and laced with Mister Harper's jabs and jokes. When the last bid was in the box belonged to Jeff Rayette.

The next morning Vera Lee looked at the front of Harper's store and smiled. The soft breeze carried the smell of a fresh mowed meadow. A cross breeze carried the pungent smell of a meadow fertilized with chicken litter. Jerking the truck door open she headed for the store.

The Coca Cola sign over the door had been hanging crooked ever since she could remember. The orange crush sign on the door was faded beyond recognition. The little bell hanging over the door still played the same little tune that had interrupted a thousand of Mr. Harper's naps.

Harper came up off the gray shorts feed bag that had taken on his exact image. "Come in here!" He commanded dropping his feet off the edge of the counter.

"Been in love with me since the day I was born? Huh," Vera Lee had a mischievous smile on her face. She proceeded to the spit and whittle chairs and plopped into one.

"I sure have. You've been like a Granddaughter to me. Do you remember those peppermint canes I slipped to you when you were a button?" They both laughed.

"I've stopped by to see if I could talk you into going to work for me. You know I'm opening a hog house through the Smokey Hill Meat Co. I need a general manager. I'm offering you the job." Vera Lee sat to wait for the full import of this to strike Mr. Harper.

This was a bolt from the blue. It was the last thing Mr. Harper expected. He dropped into a chair opposite the one Vera Lee sat in. Rubbing his face he stared at the floor. Was she serious? How long would the job last? Swarms of questions sprang up in his mind.

"I just don't know. I've never run a hog house before. I don't know all that much about hogs. I … I …" Mister Harper stuttered.

"You don't have to know much about hogs. I have hired a man who knows that end of the business. He will serve as foreman, under your watchful eye, and boss the crew actually handling the care of the hogs. Smokey Hill will select and deliver the pigs. They will select and deliver the feed. Smokey Hill will pick up the finished hogs. They will give you on the job training if you want them to.

"You're a good bookkeeper, you're a hard worker, proud of the job you do and you're honest. What I want is for you to stay on those books and keep everyone else honest. I know you will do your best to do the job right.

"This is a full time job. It would mean you have to close the store. And devote full time to the job." Vera Lee thought this might be the biggest sticking point.

Squeak; squeak the rocking chair laid a tune in the still air while Mr. Harper weighed the different options available to him at this point.

Thump! Mister Harper's feet stopped the rocker, "The roads are getting better. The cars are being improved and run faster. People have more money. There has been a large grocery store built in both of the towns east and west of us.

"These large stores buy in big bulk lots so they can buy cheap and sell at prices less than I have to pay for stuff.

"We have electricity in the valley now. Most near everyone has a freezer and a refrigerator. The people buy food in bulk and store it. Dave took away my sugar sales. Business has been awfully slow here lately.

"I've been thinking about closing the store anyway. By golly I'll do it. When do I start?"

"It will be a little while, I have to get the hog house built first. Hang in here and sell your inventory off before you close." Vera Lee was on her way to the door. On the way home her mind was swirling around the hog house she was going to build with a cellar to hide the whiskey still underneath it.

"That is a big cellar." The man studied the plans Vera Lee handed him. "It covers a lot of square feet and is well ventilated. The roof is extra strong. It will be expensive to build."

"I plan to grow root crops. The reason I'm hiring an outside contractor is I don't want the neighbors to know the cellar is there. If they know I have a big cellar they will run over every time it rains. I don't want that. It interferes with my work. If you take this job no marked truck will bring workers or material in to do the cellar work.

"We will build a pond where the big spring is on the side of the hill above and behind the house. This will cover the men and equipment you bring in. The pond will have a cement spillway. This will cover the cement work on the cellar.

Your crews are not to stay overnight in the valley or stop at the local stores. I want this cellar built quick and built right. If none of the local people know this cellar is here a year after you finish it you will get a bonus." Vera Lee crossed her arms and glared adamantly.

Under Vera Lee's watchful supervision work on the cellar progressed rapidly. Two weeks later she put a final inspection on the cellar and pond. It was a tired Vera Lee who washed up at the outside basin and sauntered into the kitchen. "Is supper ready?" she asked.

"Yes, Louis was here looking for you. He got out of prison a few days ago." Mother set the table.

YES! This was a missing part of the plan working around in Vera Lee's head.

Bright and early the next morning Vera Lee walked into the back of the corn crib, pushed on the wall. A door opened into a short tunnel leading into the cellar. The place was bright and airy. Both Rayette boys were sitting at a table in the corner with a large piece of butcher paper strung across it.

Vera lee crossed the open space and seated herself at the table. She studied the plans hand drawn on the paper.

"We have room for two stills," Junior said. "We can produce about 500 gallon per week. The hog house should cover the smell of that much mash. We can and will build the stills."

"You must be very, very careful getting the parts to build the still." Vera Lee's finger traced the lines across the paper. "We don't want to rouse any suspicion."

"Aw heck, Junior and I can make most of the stuff we need. We'll be real careful purchasing the rest. We'll be ready to run a batch off before the hog house is finished."

"Don't do anything until the feed souring barrels began to operate for the hog house. The hog house is scheduled to be finished and go into operation when the first hogs arrive in two weeks." Vera Lee said.

"We'll be ready," Junior smiled and shook his head. "It's going to be strange, working with a hundred squealing pigs over your head."

"As thick as the floor of that hog house is you will never hear them," Vera Lee laughed. "You boys better make some good stuff or I'll pull the plug between you and that manure lagoon next door."

CHAPTER 3

"Welcome home," Vera Lee hugged Louis. "It's good to be back. There have been a lot of changes since I left." Louis waved her toward a seat.

"Yeah, Dave and the revenuers have caused quite a stir in the valley." Vera Lee seated herself.

"I'll never forget that black car. He was on me so quick I couldn't get away. He pushed me off the road into a cottonmouth swamp." Louis laughed.

"What are you going to do now that you're home again?"

"I think I'll try to get on with the timber company. That is about all the work there is around here."

Louis was resigned,

"I'm going to need a driver." Vera Lee said. "Not immediately but soon. Meanwhile I'm buying a log truck and putting it to work for the timber company. Would you drive moonshine for me and drive the log truck between loads."

"Where will you get the mountain dew? I don't have a car anymore. They took mine when they caught me." Louis was interested in spite of himself. "Where would I go with the stuff? The Revenuers have caught all the people I used to do business with."

"Let me take care of the details. The less anyone knows the safer you will be. I have the logging contract and I bought a truck yesterday. You can start hauling logs tomorrow if you wish."

Vera Lee glanced at the newspaper laying on the pickup seat beside her. She'd diligently checked newspapers from various cities for ads about bakeries for sale. She needed a bakery to cover the purchase of the large amounts of sugar the whisky stills the Rayette brothers were building needed to operate

This was one bakery on which she could handle the purchase price, perhaps she could jew them down some.

Medlock, Texas, population 8,214, the sign slid silently past the window of the Chevy pickup. Vera Lee picked up the legal pad on the seat and verified the address of the Monarch Real Estate co. Satisfied her memory was correct she tossed the pad back onto the seat and piloted the pickup down the next off ramp.

"We have one bakery listed. It is on the outskirts of town. We've had it for a considerable amount of time. I have the paperwork you requested. I fear the bakery has been struggling for sometime now. The owners inherited the bakery and lives in another state. They've lowered the asking price considerably.

"There is a quite a large piece of land with the deal. There is forty acres of land no one uses right now." Ruby Rail, the real estate agent, leaned back to wait for Vera Lee's answer.

"I see Wal-Mart has built a new store on the opposite side of town. The city is growing in the opposite direction. Can you see any demand for that piece of waste land with the bakery in the near future?" Vera Lee sat back to wait for an answer.

"Honestly no, a year or so ago there was a rumor that one of the major food processing companies were considering putting a large processing plant in the area to take advantage of produce the local farmers are growing. Unfortunately the company squashed the rumor." Ruby thumbed through the paperwork.

"Would it be possible to lease this land to someone?" Vera Lee wondered.

"We have tried that and there were no takers." Ruby smiled picking up the papers. "Let's go see the bakery." She suggested.

The town seemed healthy and growing. Vera Lee noted as they drove across it. The houses were neat, and the lawns were mowed. Streets were clean and in good repair.

The bakery was the last building on the edge of town. It was built on the front corner of the forty acres next to the town. A neatly mowed lawn surrounded the bakery.

The rest of the forty acres lay in a state of total disrepair. Weeds and brush covered the entire expanse. It had been many years since this land produced anything. Trash covered the area. The sunlight winked and blinked with reflections when the wind waved the Texas wildflowers (Plastic bags) hanging in many of the bushes.

The bakery itself was a warm pleasant surprise. The wholesome aroma of fresh baked goods assailed her nose the instant the door opened. The place was spotless. Display case glasses were clean and the baked goods were displayed in an appealing manner. There were two tables in one end of the lobby where customers could sit and eat their purchases if they so desired.

"I'll be right with you." A curvaceous neatly dressed pretty dark haired young lady of twenty-five said as she placed a tray of donuts in one of the display cases. Then she said, "Oh," when she straightened and saw Ruby Rail.

"I'm Vera Lee Marley," holding out her hand she

stepped forward.

"I'm Robin Kowlowsky." Robin's handshake was firm and she looked Vera Lee in the eye.

"Robin Kowloose a what? How about if I just call you Robin," Vera Lee stumbled and they both laughed.

"Most people just call me Robin. Not many can handle the Kowlowsky part." Robin didn't appear to resent Vera Lee's stumble at pronouncing her last name.

Vera lee inspected the rest of the bakery. The place was clean; the appliances were of good brands and appeared to be in good working order.

The supply room was a disappointment. There was a definite shortage of supplies. There wasn't much of anything in the room.

On the way out Vera Lee paused in front of Robin, "How about I buy you dinner this evening to make up for butchering your name?"

Robin weighed the invitation. Why was it offered? "I suppose so. Where do you want to eat?"

"Your town, I'm sure you know the right place to

eat." Vera Lee smiled.

Ruby Rail scowled but remained silent. She resented the fact she had not been invited to this dinner and wondered what purpose it could have in the possible transaction.

"Ok, I close at five. I'll meet you at the Yellow Rose Café at six. Ruby can show you where it is on the way back to the office."

Vera Lee gathered the papers from the desk in the office Ruby loaned her and walked into Ruby's office. She had spent considerable time studying and understanding them. She sat in a chair in front of Ruby's desk and tossed the paper work on the desk.

"There has been no profit this year. The place has barely been breaking even. Some months it hasn't been breaking even."

Ruby steepled her hands in front of her and rested her elbows on the desk. A pen dangled between her fingers. "That's right but I think with a good manager it could do better. The man who owns it now is struggling to keep it open so he can get the most money he can out of it. He trusts no one. He is very cautious and he lives in another state."

"This property is a pain in the butt to him. It is making him no money and taking time and money to run it. I'll bet the city is on him about the condition of the forty acres also. It will be quite expensive to clean it." Vera Lee surmised.

Ruby nodded. Perhaps Vera Lee wasn't as much a country bumpkin as she had thought her to be.

"Offer him half what he is asking and we'll see how much he wants be loose from this problem he has. All this will be done in my mother's maiden name, Ruth Stiller. I have a power of attorney and I'm acting in her behalf."

Robin was walking to the Café door when Vera Lee arrived. They chose a booth in the corner where they could talk without anyone listening to or interrupting the conversation.

At first the conversation was drifting and general. They were feeling each other out and getting to know something about each other.

"Granny Whooten built the bakery just to have

something to do. After Gramps passed away she moved down here to be with mother and other relatives. She lived at a place called Frogville. It's somewhere up in Oklahoma. Granny could bake anything and she was so lonesome after Gramps passed away.

"You saw the tables in the bakery. Every morning a group of old ladies had their coffee with Granny Whooten. Granny didn't care if the bakery made a lot of money or not. It was something to do and a link to our family and friends.

"I don't know why Granny left the bakery to Uncle Joe. The first thing he did was tell her friends not to come back for morning coffee. He said a group of old ladies sitting around might upset a potential buyer. The real problem with Uncle Joe was that Granny didn't charge her friends for the coffee they drank. He's a skinflint."

"I noticed you're woefully short on baking supplies," Vera Lee's tone made it a question.

"That's my skinflint Uncle. He's afraid someone will buy the joint and demand the supplies go with the place. He won't buy enough supplies to keep up with demand. I'm sure if we had the supplies we could make it a profitable operation."

"How sure are you it could be made profitable? Are you sure enough to gamble some of your time and effort on the project?" Vera Lee smiled.

"What are you talking about?" Robin was at a loss.

"If I buy the bakery and hire you as manager would you take the profit for the first six months as your wages?" Vera Lee saw shock register in Robin's eyes.

"Me the manager?" Robin sat silent for a time. "Would I be manager or would you order all the supplies?"

"You will be manager as long as you can keep the bakery at a profitable level. The profit is all the pay you will receive for the first six months. I will be looking over your shoulder but you run the place." Vera Lee paused folding a napkin and then continued.

"There is one thing with the supplies. I have another store. I'll want to order all the supplies through this bakery. I can get sugar, yeast and so forth at a much lower rate if I buy in big lots. The stuff I take to the other store will not be charged to the profit or loss of the bakery here in Medlock.

"You will be manager for the first six months. We will negotiate your continuation as manager and wages at that point. Naturally the higher the profit levels of the bakery the higher your salary will be." Vera Lee sat back to let Robin think.

"I've never heard of a deal like this. It's wacky. I'm sure I can make more money this way than Uncle Joe ever paid me. There are a couple of accounts I'm sure I can get if I'm allowed to operate with a free hand. I'm going to take you up on it." Robin stuck a hand out to shake on the deal.

"All we have to do now is convince Uncle Joe to sell us the place at a reasonable rate." Vera Lee began gathering her stuff to leave. It was long drive home.

The house was spotless when Vera Lee entered. Ruth was sitting in her rocking chair. There was no needle in her hand. A big smile lit her face when

Vera Lee entered.

"WOW! You must be feeling better." Vera Lee hugged her mother and kissed her forehead.

"You were gone when I woke up this morning. You have been gone all day. What is this young fellow's name?"

Vera Lee grinned. Mother was nothing if not persistent. "I was on farm business today. But who knows. It could happen someday."

"Supper is ready and a lady named Ruby Rail sent word. She needs you to sign some papers." Mother was on the way to put supper on the table. "By the way Billy Jack came home today. He got out early because of good behavior or some silly thing."

Vera Lee settled into the rocker her mother vacated. Three Whippoorwills tuned up in the road in front of the gate. Their 'Jack married the widow' calls echoed off the barn. A great horned owl sent a soft, where are you, call to his mate. Another piece of the plan was taking shape. She would find Billy Jack tomorrow.

The cloud of dust the red pickup pulled along

behind it rolled over and enveloped the cab when Vera Lee slowed to turn into the trail leading to Billy Jack's house. The fields were overgrown with weeds and small bushes. The fences sagged here and there. It never ceased to amaze Vera Lee as to how fast nature reclaimed land that wasn't cared for.

The house and barn were in worse shape than the fields. Billy Jack sat on the porch. "Get out and join the party!" He waved at Vera Lee.

Vera Lee opened the door and looked through the tall grass and weeds for a Copperhead before she stepped down. "Welcome home. I thought there would be a bunch of people here."

"I told everyone I wanted to get over the shock of seeing the old place alone. "

The gate post served as a secure resting place and allowed Vera Lee to avoid sitting on the dusty porch.

The conversation ran along politely for some time then Billy Jack placed both feet on the ground. "The Vera Lee I went to school with had something on her mind when she had that look on her face," Billy Jack smiled.

"Oh, you watched my face then?

"I sure did, but all you could see was David Maloy. What's on your mind?" Billy Jack leaned against the porch post and waited.

"I'm taking over Daddy's customers and I'm going to move a lot of whiskey north. I need your help. I have built a sawmill at the Barnes Furniture Factory at Penwick, Nebraska. I need a good man to run the mill. This man will run the mill, saw and sell lumber to the factory and distribute the dew as it comes in." Vera Lee waited for an answer.

"I don't have a car and I'm so out of practice I couldn't handle it if I had one." Billy Jack looked at his boot toes and scratched his head.

"The days of the fast cars and whistling bullets are over." Vera Lee stated emphatically. "If you take this job you will be mostly working the mill and delivering lumber. Once a week you will deliver the shine to a location. A different location each week and then you will call a telephone number I give you. You will never deliver to the same place two times in a row. You will never see the people who pick up the shine and they won't know who you are or where you are going to deliver until you have delivered and left."

"How will the shine get to me?"

"Are you going to take the job?" Vera Lee questioned.

Billy Jack looked around disgustedly. "There's not much around here for an

Ex-convict. At least up north no one will know I'm an ex-con. Yes, I want the job."

"The shine will come up on the log truck with the logs you will be sawing. Louis will be driving the truck. The truck has been modified. The back halves of the fuel tanks have been modified to hold shine. A tank has been built into the back of the cab and there will be two huge hollow oak trees full of shine in the log load. All together there will be about five hundred gallons of shine per load.

"The truck should be able to stand a pretty stiff inspection without anything being detected." Vera paused for a breath. "Louis has already hauled several loads of logs to the mill. He has been getting the highway patrol and local police in the small towns used to seeing logs going north. There is no shine there yet so get your sawmill going and I'll get back to you."

"I don't have the means to get to Nebraska." Billy Jack said.

"I'll send you up with Louis in the truck with a load of logs. We're very short on money right now. We'll have to stretch it until we get paid for the first run."

During the next weeks Vera Lee was everywhere hurrying operations along. With the duties at the farm and the other obligations she slept very little. It seemed everything was moving in slow motion. No matter how hard she tried or how hard she pushed delays arose at every turn.

Late for supper again, Vera Lee dragged her tired body to the table. The quiet was oppressing. The only sounds were the soft rattling of pans as mother reheated Vera Lee's supper. Vera Lee sat her elbows on the table and lowering her face into her hands she rested her eyes.

"Some lady named Ruby Rail sent you a note and said she needed to talk to you soon. It is regarding the forty acres of land you bought at Medlock, Texas." Mother slid the plate of reheated food across the table and seated herself in her usual place at the end of the table. Vera poked at the food with a fork. She was too tired to eat.

If the town council wants that forty acres cleaned up, let them do it, Vera Lee thought. *I'm not going to worry about it right now.*

"Why did you buy land so far away? There is no way you can work it." Mother was curious.

"It seemed like good idea at the time. It is an investment." Vera Lee was elated. Mother was coming out of the semi-comatose state she shrank into when Jason went to prison.

A slow smile crossed Vera Lee's face. What would Mother say if she knew the bakery was deeded to her maiden name and had been purchased to cover the purchase of sugar and yeast for the whisky still?

The smile started with Vera Lee's lips and eventually worked its way into her eyes. Carving off a small slice of the meat Vera Lee tasted it. Suddenly she was hungry and fell to with a will.

"I'll take care of Ruby when I pay bills after supper." Vera Lee rounded up a fork full of mashed potatoes.

Mother remained silent. She was not sure what she did, but she knew that whatever she said cheered her little princess up. This was enough. Folding her napkin she dropped it into her lap.

Vera Lee sat before her thinking dresser with a brush in her hands. Bills were piling up and demands for payment growing sharper each day. There was no income to pay the bills.

The day finally came when all was in operation. Vera Lee chose to open the paperwork from the bakery first.

Robin's report was cheerful. The bakery sales were up. Robin made a deal with FARMER'S, a large grocery store, to sell bakery items in the store. Vera Lee looked back through the paper work from the bakery. She could find no mention of a needed cleanup of the forty acres. The news was all encouraging. Everything was operating but not bringing in enough to pay the bills.

The bakery, the hog barn, the logging operation, the Sawmill and the whiskey still were all operating.

The Rayette brothers finished their first run on the still and the product had been delivered to Cleo up north. With the first load delivered it was payoff time. Some of the mounting bills could be paid off.

Days past without any word or money from the load of whiskey that went north. Vera Lee was beginning to think perhaps Cleo, the middleman, was going to fail to pay.

The phone buzzed on and on. No answer. Vera Lee slammed it back on the cradle. This was the third time she had driven into town to reach the middleman at his car dealership. Once he was out and once was with a customer. He had not returned any of her calls. The drives into town to make these calls were cutting into her work time and costing her gas money she could not afford.

"What do I do now?" Vera Lee asked herself.

The other operations were in the beginning stages. Nothing much could be expected of them for sometime to come.

The collection notices were becoming sharper and more often. Vera Lee was sifting through the mail when a letter bearing the name of the company she bought fuel

from caught her eye. Reluctantly she broke the seal and anxiously scanned the contents. No more fuel until present accounts were settled.

The chair squeaked when she settled into it and the tears rolled. After her initial out break of tears she moved to her thinking mirror.

Vera Lee sat in front of the mirror and yanked the comb through her hair. Ledger books adorned the floor where they landed when she angrily swept them off the dresser. All the money was gone! She was broke! All the money was gone.

CHAPTER 4

All Daddies' money was gone! How could she face him? How could she explain to him that she'd spent all the money he had worked for and saved on a wild hair brained scheme that didn't work? What could she do? She'd tried so hard. What would she do with mother and herself?

She had been so brash as to mortgage the farm. Daddy had signed for this but she talked him into it. Things seemed to be working at the time. She dropped her head again. She was physically and emotionally exhausted.

Folding her arms she laid them on the dresser and lowered her forehead to her rest on her arms and let the tears roll.

Mother came in with the mail. She looked at Vera Lee and laid the mail down. Walking away mother looked back, "Ruby Rail came again today. I told her you were busy but she said tell you it was important you call her."

Vera Lee raised her head, nodded, and pushed the mail mother placed on the dresser away. She needed no more bills at this time. When she withdrew her hand she noticed the top letter was from the timber company Louis and her truck were hauling for. What kind of bill could they be sending her? Curiously she opened it. It was a check for last period's operations. It was not a large check but it was definitely a check.

Fishing around she found the letter from the fuel company. The timber check was large enough to cover the fuel bills. She read the rest of the mail. There was also a small check from the furniture manufacturer. It wasn't much but it was a few days reprieve.

Vera Lee stared into the mirror. The black eyes

grew harder and harder. Her shoulders rose and the slump came out of her back.

Moving to the window she watched the fire flies doing their mating dance and listened to the Whippoorwills talking to the soft darkness of the night. A cricket tuned up on the window sill. The sweet scent of wild honeysuckle drifted through the open window. "This is my valley," she vowed, "There is no way I'm going to leave it."

Walking resolutely to the closet Vera Lee removed Jason's snub nosed .38 special. Checking to be sure it was loaded she dropped it and a box of hollow point bullets into her purse. If she was going down she would go out in a blaze of glory and she was going to have company on her way to hell! She headed north.

The black thunderstorm cloud was moving toward the highway. A bright tongue of lightening kept flicking from the leading edge to strike the dry grass of the prairie. A wall of water was falling behind it. Vera Lee took a sip of coffee. Driving across wide open spaces like this great prairie always made her sleepy. Checking her watch she dropped her speed five miles per hour. She wanted to arrive at the auto dealership at closing time.

Cleo finished the paperwork and slammed the book closed. Looking around he smiled. This had been a profitable week. The first load of Mountain Dew had been delivered and sold. The money was resting in his safe.

The sight of this money was almost more than he could bear. He was supposed to deposit payment for the dew into a special account set up for Vera Lee but the avarice in his soul wouldn't let him do it.

After all she was just a woman. A cold eyed beautiful woman but she was still a woman. He'd cheated many ladies of this type in his years of dealing used cars. Why not just take one big profit and be out of it.

This was his favorite time of day. The place was deserted and quiet. Taking the ring of keys from the center drawer of his desk he rose and walked to the front door.

Before he reached the door he realized someone was standing inside leaning against the door.

"I'm sorry we're closed," Cleo automatically used his smooth car salesman's voice.

"Not quite, we need to talk." Vera Lee stepped forward.

"Oh," Cleo recognized her. "We'll have to talk later. I have a dinner engagement. I suppose you want to talk about money. I have been so busy I couldn't get over to deposit it as planned. I'll do it tomorrow. I must go now."

Vera Lee Stepped out of the shadows and handed Cleo a brief case.

"What is this for?" Cleo opened the lid to see what was inside. The case was empty.

"If my money don't go into that brief case you will never eat another dinner." Vera Lee's voice was quiet and cold. The black eyes speared Cleo. He was like a rat caught in the glare of a rattler. His brain wanted to run but his feet wouldn't move.

"I ... I..." he stuttered. Then he heard the distinctive clicks of a Colt revolver being drawn to full cock. His eyes went to the hand in Vera Lee's jacket pocket.

"I have your money over here in the safe. We'll go get it." He stated to turn.

"Hold it," Vera Lee ordered. "This thing has a hair trigger. If you try to get cute

it will blow holes in you I can stick my fist through. If anything comes out of that safe besides money your whole evening will be spoiled."

Cleo fumbled with the combination on the safe. He kept looking over his shoulder hoping Vera Lee didn't get nervous and shake with her finger on the trigger. That hand was rock solid and the animosity in those eyes burned his skin.

"We've been busy. Honestly, I would not cheat you." Cleo spun the dial again to clear his bumbling attempt at the combination. "I was going to deposit your money tomorrow. Honest, I really was."

"Stop!" Vera Lee ordered. "You don't want to get me thinking you're stalling with that combination do you?" The hand slid out of her pocket and the black hole of death looked squarely into the close space between Cleo's eyes. His stomach leaped up and grabbed his throat, his skin crawled, He could feel the big bullet breaking bone and smashing vital organs. Bile boiled up and filled his mouth with a bitter taste.

At their first meeting Cleo thought this lady was coldly beautiful. Now she was the picture of death. Standing with feet spread, the feral gleam flowing from those dark eyes was like pouring ice water over him. He shivered.

The skin on her face was drawn tight by the thin line of her mouth. The smile of death was plastered on her face.

As a matter of fact Vera Lee was scared to death. Fear was the reason she stood so stiff. This was out of and far beyond her league, but this was daddy's money. This was her and her mother's living. There was no way this lowlife scumbag was going to take Daddy's money and her life style away. Feeling there was nothing left and no other way out she was a woman acting out of sheer desperation. This made her a very dangerous person indeed. She would pull the trigger if necessary.

Cleo carefully rolled the dial in the right combination this time. Twisting the handle he opened the safe door. A pistol lay in the right back corner of the safe. If he could get to it and have any luck he could say she was robbing him.

Another look at Vera Lee's face sent thoughts of the pistol thundering from his mind like a covey of startled quail. If she is this calm she had confidence in her abilities. This is not the first time she has did this, he thought. Stop shaking and get on with it.

Carefully placing his right hand on top of the safe where Vera Lee could see it he stacked the bills into the briefcase with his left hand until all the money was transferred from the safe to the briefcase. Pushing the door shut he took the briefcase and rose.

Motioning toward his desk she said, "Place the briefcase on the desk and sit in that chair against the wall." A relieved look was easing into Vera Lee's eyes. Cleo's composure was returning. "You have the wrong Idea Miss," he said in a soothing voice.

"There's no way I'd cheat you. I'm real sorry I didn't get that money deposited as planned. I suppose this misunderstanding has called our deal off?" He eased himself into the chair against the wall.

Vera Lee leaned against the desk in thought. "Not necessarily." She said. "I had just as soon deal with one crook as another. The boy's wanted to come visit you this time. But I can't trust their discretion. After the long drive up here they would have wanted to leave a few marks on your hide so you would remember they had been here." Vera Lee lied easily.

"Two things to remember", Vera slid the pistol back into her jacket pocket. The boys know where I am and who you are." Vera Lee lied again. "If me and this briefcase don't get home they will come to find out where we went. I surely would hate to have any trouble on the highway. It would be very unhealthy for you. You sit in that chair for five minutes and you will be able to apologize to your dinner companions for being late."

Leaving the car dealership Vera Lee drove

toward the interstate until she was out of sight and then turned onto a residential street. Crossing a residential section of town she took an obscure little state highway that ended in Penwick, Nebraska.

Once she was clear of town Vera Lee stopped at a roadside table. Removing a bundle of the money she placed the briefcase in a strong cardboard box and taped it heavily. The box already had her home address and the proper amount of postage on it.

When Billy Jack opened the mill the next morning a red pickup was parked behind a stack of lumber.

"Hey gorgeous!" Jack thumped on the cab.

Vera Lee sat up in the seat and rubbing her eyes lowered the window.

"What are you doing here and why are you sleeping in the mill yard?" Billy Jack was puzzled.

"I'm just passing through. I wanted to eat breakfast with you and it was too late to rent a motel. Hop in. I have to go by the post office and mail this package then we'll find a place to eat." Vera Lee was still waking up.

"Sorry beautiful, I don't see how any man could

turn down that offer but in the first place I just finished breakfast and I'm behind on orders for lumber. It seems our oak lumber is superior to what they've been getting. We're not only selling Barnes all their oak. Leland furniture is buying all the lumber I can saw beyond Barn's needs.

I'm not giving Leland or anyone else the discount you gave Barnes. I figure if we have better lumber they should pay for it.

"I'm going to have to hire help and you're going to have to send Louis up more often." Jack ran out of wind.

Vera Lee sat thumping the steering wheel. The restless prairie wind spun little dust clouds across the mill yard. This was a positive development with possibilities. "I'll make a deal with you." Vera Lee finally spoke. "You take me to breakfast and I'll work with you at the mill for the rest of the day. We can discuss the future of the mill."

Billy Jack flipped the lock up and opened the door, "Scoot over, I drive."

Vera Lee actually enjoyed working with Billy Jack

at the mill. She pulled her weight and listened to his ideas. It was apparent he was going to need a bigger mill soon and help to run it. Where was the money to do this going to come from?

If she started Louis hauling more hardwood to this mill she was going to need another log truck and driver to fill her contract with the timber company.

If the need grew she would have to purchase more hardwood timber. In time the Marley timberlands will be depleted. Where would this money come from? Money, money, everything revolved around money.

I have the money from the first load of moonshine. Will there be another load? She thought. *There has to be.*

We'll stay with Cleo, god bless his crooked little weaseling used car dealer soul, Vera Lee smiled, *we can handle him if he lets his greed override his good sense again.*

The mile markers went by with monotonous regularity. She kept a sharp eye on the rear view mirror and the traffic around her. She didn't think Cleo would send anyone after her but she was still being very watchful. Nothing happened worse than the soft spatter of the bugs on the windshield.

She was exhausted when Jack limped to the gate to bay his welcome home to her. An old hen clucked her way past the gate. All ten of her little yellow fluff balls had to run to keep up.

"Well," Mother was indignant. "You finally made it home. Where have you been and what is his name?"

"I told you I was on farm business. I'm trying to get more for our products." Vera Lee was weary.

"Huh, in my day young ladies didn't run around and stay gone from home for days on end." Mother turned back. "That Ruby Rail lady is here. She has a motel room in town. I told her you might be home tonight. She's coming back. She said she had to talk to you."

"In your day all a young lady had to do was look pretty and marry someone who took care of her. I have to make us a living. What does Ruby Rail want anyway? Tell her I'm exhausted and I'll see her tomorrow." Vera Lee was getting irked.

Vera Lee was eating breakfast when Jack greeted Ruby Rail at the gate. Vera Lee rose to greet Ruby and lead her into the office out of Mother's hearing. "What is so important," Vera Lee demanded grumpily.

"Well," Ruby laid her briefcase on Vera Lee's desk and opened it. "You remember us discussing the big produce company that thought about building a processing plant where the bakery is? They didn't back out. They were quietly purchasing the land needed. They have all the land they need except the forty acres you own. It seems we beat them to it when you purchased the bakery."

"They have taken my inability to reach you as the sign of negotiation for a higher price. They have sweetened the price they are offering a couple times.

"The reason I'm here is that they are growing short on patience. I'm afraid they will come up with another way to build their factory without buying the forty acres. And another reason I'm here is that I want to represent you in your negotiations with them." Ruby removed a paper from the briefcase and handed it to Vera Lee.

Vera Lee took the paper and glanced at it. She

did a double take and feeling for the chair arm sat down. The offer for the forty acres was far more money than she had owned when she started this project.

Stunned, Vera Lee reread the proposal. This would replace Daddy's money! She could pay off the mortgage on the farm and still have most of Daddy's money left. "I see they have cut the one acre the bakery sits on out of the deal. I'd actually be selling thirty nine acres. I do want to keep the bakery."

"I took the privilege of getting that into the offer. This land will be zoned A 1 commercial. That acre will be valuable.

If the land is not so zoned, there will be a big demand for housing after the processing plant is built. You could sub-divide the acre into lots and do well on it." Ruby removed more papers from her briefcase. "I drew up these papers in hope you would retain me to represent you during the negotiations. If this is what you want we will need you to sign them."

Six months later Vera Lee closed the ledger books with a sigh of contentment. The money from the sale of the land gave her enough operating capitol to bring the other projects to full operation and maintain a respectable operating capitol.

Vera Lee took up her brush and moved to the window. The fire flies and whippoorwills were gone. They had found their mates, raised their young and took them home to their winter grounds. They would return another year. Old Jack had gone to doggy heaven where the fox were slow and arthritis didn't exist.

The tree leaves were turning to red, gold and soft brown. Vera Lee drew the brush slowly and thoughtfully through her hair.

Daddy was so proud of his little girl. It was a pleasure to visit the prison and bask the sunshine of his admiration. Jason promised her he would be on his best behavior with an eye to the possibility of early parole.

Mother climbed out of the shell she enclosed herself in when Jason went to prison. She was keeping the house unassisted and visiting with old friends and members of the community.

Returning to the dresser she took a seat in front of the mirror. Early on she converted the spare bedroom to an office. It was equipped with the usual desk, rolling chairs and file cabinets but her favorite place to think and plan was brushing her hair in front of the mirror in her bedroom.

Whoa! It dawned on her she had not thought about David Miloy since she entered the room. Not even when she looked out the window had the old feelings raised their ugly head.

The top ledger book pertained to the bakery. She and Robin agreed on a fair wage and Robin agreed to stay on as manager. Absently she flipped to the last entries.

The bakery was doing great. Robin's deal with the display in the grocery store had since grown into a display deal with several of the big outlet stores. Sales had climbed steadily since she purchased the bakery.

The construction gangs building the food

processing plant turned the little bakery itself into a gold mine. The profits grew larger every week.

Robin re-instituted the Granny Whooten coffee club. When the business began making a solid profit she not only gave free coffee to the Granny Whooten club members, she extended it to free donuts as well. Robin felt like Granny Whooten was sitting there smiling every morning.

To the construction workers it like getting to see their Grannies every morning. To some it was seeing their Granny every morning. There was much good natured banter flying back and forth. Both the construction workers and the Grannies loved it.

Closing the Bakery book she opened the hog house books again. She had entered this industry at the right time. Smokey Hill Meat was expanding rapidly. They had taken Mr. Harper under their wing. With his natural abilities and their assistance he had the hog house running at maximum capacity. Yesterday she received and deposited a check from Smokey Hill Meat that would have taken her breath away six months ago.

Closing the hog house books she dragged the mill books over. These represented little more than reports on the operations. Billy Jack had assumed full control over this operation. He purchased the lots the mill sat on and built a new modern mill on the site.

After a few months operation Billy Jack purchased the Barnes Furniture Factory.

Vera Lee hired a full time timber locater and purchasing agent to keep the mill supplied. The majority of the loads of hardwood going north had no shine in them.

Vera Lee and Billy Jack coordinated this operation through long telephone conversations and an increasing number of long business dinners.

Mother grew increasingly suspicious and was constantly questioning. Vera Lee grew more adroit at avoiding the questions.

The logging operation for the Timber Company had grown to five trucks.

The legitimate companies she had set up to cover her bootlegging operation were making as much money as the whiskey still.

The whiskey still was doing fine. Cleo, God rest his greedy little soul, had gotten the message. He could see her rise to power and feared her more every day. Every penny due was deposited into the proper account promptly.

She pushed the books back and looked at her watch. She was due at a board meeting for the local youth summer camp. She donated heavily to the camp. She made sure no child was turned away due to the lack of funds.

Mother and Vera Lee occupied their pew in church every Sunday. They attended every public meeting in the valley. Vera Lee donated to all the local charities. She reclaimed her position as a leader in the valley. She was very smooth and had no trouble interacting with Dave and Lesa Maloy.

CHAPTER 5

"Turn right onto the next street." Rudy hooked a finger in his long hair, placed it behind his ear and studied the hand drawn map in his hands. "Yeah, that's Cheyenne Road." Rudy again turned to the map in his hand, "There is an irrigation pumping station one mile down this road. Our stuff will be stacked against the back wall."

"I see the light on the pump station. Are you sure we had to buy ten cases of quart jars?" Clyde wheeled the old blue Ford pickup onto Cheyenne Road.

"Yep, this outfit won't sell any less. I talked Jamal into putting up half of the money. We won't be stuck with it all. This outfit makes good moonshine. I drank some yesterday." Rudy leaned out the window looking for any kind of trap. He was always nervous at a pickup point.

The pump station loomed up out of the dark. Clyde wheeled the wheezing Ford around and when the lights hit the back of the pump station, there she sat. Ten boxes of quart fruit jars stacked against the wall with a flimsy plastic tarp thrown over them.

Leaping from the truck Rudy tossed the tarp aside and fumbled at the box opening. He pulled a quart jar of crystal clear liquid from the box. The liquid sparkled in the glow of the headlight. Shaking the jar Rudy watched in fascination as small beads formed and rose toward the top of the jar.

"Hoowee! These jars are plumb full," Rudy cradled the jar like a baby and danced a jig. Clyde slid out of the driver's seat and left the door open. He surveyed the surrounding territory thoroughly. He remained watchful. He still worried about the Revenue Agents.

Walking past the cavorting Rudy Clyde pulled several of the jars up high enough to see the contents.

"All the jars are full," Clyde examined another box. "We'll take a little bit from each jar and keep it to drink."

This thought stopped Rudy in his tracks. "You mean free drinks?" he asked unbelieving.

"Yeah we'll take exactly two ounces out of each jar. That will keep them all looking alike. They will all be the same amount of full. No one will notice and if they do we'll tell them that is the way they were when we got them." Clyde said.

Rudy sat the jar on top of the box and began counting on his fingers. "Twelve jars to the case …, one hundred twenty jars …, two ounces per jar …," Rudy could barely count his fingers and toes but when it came to drinking whiskey he was willing to put the effort there.

"Holy Mackerel Man!! That's over one and three quarter gallon of free whiskey. I'm going to get me a drink right now!" Rudy reached for the jar.

"No! We have to take exactly two ounces from each jar. Each jar has to have exactly the same amount in it. You know half of this is Jamal's. We have to get this past him as well as our customers.

"Now, help me get this loaded and let us get out of here. This place is giving me the willies. I can feel someone watching us." Clyde grabbed a case and carried it to the pickup.

Rudy stuck the quart jar inside his shirt and grabbed the case minus one jar and rushed to the truck. Turning the case he placed it so Clyde wouldn't miss the one jar.

Pulling the jar from his shirt he laid it against the seat on the floor of the Ford. He managed to do this before Clyde turned back toward the truck with another case.

The ten cases were quickly loaded and the tarp tucked in around them. Clyde pulled an envelope from the glove box.

"That is our money," Rudy objected.

"This is the money we agreed to pay for the whiskey." Clyde was puzzled.

"What if we just took off with the whiskey and the money? There's no one around." Rudy waved his hand in a circle.

Clyde shook his head, "Not me buddy!" he said emphatically. "I've heard this bunch is rough on people who tried to short arm them. As to no one watching, I told you awhile ago I feel eyes on me. I still feel them. The hair on my back is climbing up to my neck. Get in the truck. I'm going to put this money in that little wood box just like I was told to and we're going to get the heck out here!"

Five mile down the road Clyde leaned back and relaxed, "I recon we made that pickup alright. I don't see anything anywhere."

"Good," Rudy reached down and picked up the quart of whiskey. He reached for the lid.

"WHAT ARE YOU DOING?" Clyde shouted

Rudy jumped. "I'm getting me a drink," He said defiantly.

Clyde was furious. "Rudy I told you no drinks until we got everything sorted out."

"What difference does it make whether I get a drink now or wait for you to sort it out? Who died and elected you God anyway? I thought I was a partner. I'm not some hired help you can boss around." Rudy was defiant.

Clyde raised his hand to speak and saw the stop sign flash by. "Oh no!" The hand fell back into the seat.

"What are you …," Rudy began.

"I just ran a stop sign and … Oh no!" Clyde slapped the seat between them. "A set of headlights came on back there! It will be the cops! It has to be cops. Roll that window down and toss the jar way out into the weeds before they get close enough to see you do it."

"Throw good whiskey out the window? What is the matter with you? I'll set it in the floor and cover it with my legs." Rudy wasn't about to abuse good drinking whiskey.

"THROW IT OUT!!" Clyde screamed. "It is a cop! He just turned his red lights on! Get rid of it!" Clyde repeated.

Rudy looked over his shoulder at blinking red lights gaining on them rapidly. He fumbled with the lid on the jar, unscrewed it, spilled a few drops on his shirt and took a long drink from the jar. Rolling the window down he pitched the jar and remaining whiskey into the darkness.

Clyde moved the truck off the pavement into a clean place, stopped and pulled his billfold from his pocket. The car with the blinking lights slid quietly in behind them. A set of flood lights pushed the blackness of the night a little farther back.

Two Deputy Sheriffs climbed from the patrol car. Each had a long black flashlight in his hand.

The second Deputy stopped at the back left corner of the pickup. The first proceeded to the window. "May I see your driver's license and insurance card?" he asked politely. Clyde produced the required documents.

After looking at the license and insurance card the Deputy said, "Mr. Ramsey, the reason I stopped you was because you didn't even slow down for the stop sign back there."

"Yes sir, I didn't see it in time. I ran right through it," Clyde admitted. He wasn't about to argue or try to talk himself out of it. He wanted to get the ticket and get out of here.

"Have you been drinking tonight?" The young Deputy thumped the driver's license against the flashlight.

"No Sir, nothing," Clyde declared.

"I smell the strong odor of alcohol emanating from your truck. Will you step out please?" The Deputy stepped back a little.

Clyde stepped confidently out. He knew the Deputy would realize he had not been drinking.

The Deputy looked Clyde over. "Step back to the front of the patrol car please." Clyde obliged.

"Passenger, have you had anything to drink?" The young Deputy relinquished Clyde to the older, heavier deputy.

"I've had one beer," Rudy lied.

"When?"

"Aw, two or thee hours ago, our wives are waiting on us. If you have to give us a ticket please do so. We're in a hurry." Rudy tried.

"We won't be much longer. Step out and step back with your buddy. The alcohol I smell is much more recent than three hours ago. I must look in the vehicle to see if you have an open container." The Deputy motioned Rudy back to the front of the patrol car.

The Deputy shined his light around the interior of the pickup and closed the door with a satisfied grunt. Clyde let out a sigh of relief.

"Both of you put your hands on the side of the pickup," the young Deputy ordered.

"I thought you had missed it," the older Deputy chuckled as he snapped handcuffs on Clyde.

"I could see it was cases of jars by the way your light shined through that flimsy tarp. I thought it safer to get them both out and cuffed before we looked to see if that is grape cool aid in those jars."

"We'll have to call the Internal Revenue boys and turn this one over to them. You did a good job though." The veteran smiled at the rookie.

After booking Clyde and Rudy were duly passed on into the hands of the Internal Revenue Service.

"I've been sitting in this interrogation room answering your questions for four hours!" Rudy protested.

"You've told us so many lies you can't keep track of them. What's worse is I'm losing track." The tall thin Revenue Agent rose from the table. "Rudy, for the last time, If you will give me the man who made the stuff I will see you get more probation. If not you're in a fine pickle. You're not only facing charges for the illegal booze, you're facing probation violations that will keep you in the big house for a long time. Who made that moonshine?"

Rudy dropped his head and placed his hands over his face. "I don't know who made it. We picked it up just like I told you." he said softly.

"We got a call and they told us where to pick it up. We left the money in a box. I don't know who made it and I don't know who sold it to us."

Alan, the tall thin agent turned to his bald rolly-polly partner and shook his head. He then turned back to Rudy, "How did they contact you in the first place?"

"Some fellow called and asked if we wanted to buy shine and told us where to find it when I said yes." Rudy dropped his hands and leaned back.

"How were you to order more shine when this was sold?" The chunky Bart questioned for the first time.

"They will call me when more shine is available." Rudy was trying to decide which was greater, his fear of the man on the telephone line or his loathing of the jailhouse. How much of this stuff could these agents make stick and how much was bluff. This wasn't his first dance with these boys.

"Will you co-operate with us?" Alan asked. "Will you notify us of the next call? We will give you marked money to pay for the whiskey. We'd like to get a trace on the telephone call."

"Not much of a chance getting a trace on the phone. This guy is quick and slick. What you are asking me to do could be down right unhealthy. What's in it for me?" Rudy questioned.

"We will put a good word in with the District Attorney for you … "Bart started.

"No sir!" Rudy thought about the person or persons peddling the moonshine. "I want full immunity. And I mean full immunity! I want this in writing. Not one day in jail. No parole violation either. I'll have to change my name and leave here."

Alan stared at Bart for a moment. A, 'this is all we are going to get out of him,' silent communication passed between them.

"Ok, we'll take that statement under advisement. Let us talk to Clyde and see what kind of deal he will make with us. We'll get to bottom of it one way or another." Bart turned the screws a little on Rudy.

"Clyde can't tell you anything. This is my deal." Rudy handed it back to Bart.

Walking down the hall Alan turned to Bart. "As much as I hate to, we'd just as well make a deal with this scum bag. He's better than the other two we have in jail and none of them seem to know anything,"

An hour later Rudy was chattering like a magpie. He was happy. Once again he'd found a way for someone else to be punished for his wrong doings. He was going to get out of it scot free. Well, not totally scot free. He was going to have to watch for the people he was setting up.

"When someone tries to buy from you tell them

you have sold all you had but to try again you will have more. This will tell your supplier you are sold out and they will contact you." Alan handed Rudy a small box, "Keep this in your pocket it is a hand full of quarters. You do not spend these quarters for drinks or anything else. When you get a call from the bootlegger you go to the nearest pay phone and call this number. We'll try to beat him to the drop point."

Alan hooked one of his long bony fingers under Rudy's nose and pulled Rudy's head back until they were looking each other in the eye. "This deal is only as good as it comes off. If we don't get that bootlegger the deal is off and I'm going to ask the Judge for an additional five years for you." Rudy's mirth disappeared. He visibly shrank. "Don't you dare prank around with us!" Alan demanded.

"We're keeping your buddy Clyde in solitary until this operation is over. No one but you knows he's in jail. You try to get cute with me and I'll toss you in with him and lose the paperwork on both of you." Rudy had no doubt about Alan's sincerity.

Three days later Alan answered his ringing telephone. "This is Rudy. I got the call. I'm supposed to pick up twenty cases behind the little country store that went out of business out on route nine three mile west of town at 3:30 AM."

Alan was silent for a moment. "There is a gas station on the corner of route nine and route 14. This station has outdoor restrooms. Go in the restroom but don't lock the door. I will meet you there."

"What if someone sees us there" Rudy was worried,

"I'll be driving an unmarked car. No one will notice." Alan turned to Bart and smiled. He always felt better when they were planning a raid.

The door squeaked when Alan entered the rest room. "I have the money in this box count it and sign the form lying on top."

"Why should I count it? I'm going to leave it in an old wood box when I get to the Lavender market." Rudy was lazy and it was going to kill his soul to have give up all that beautiful money. There should be a way he could retain a fee out of it.

"You're going to sign for it because every cent better be there when you leave it.

Son, if every cent of that money is not there when you leave I will mow you up one side and down the other. You better count it to see if it is all there when you get it." Alan was getting annoyed.

"The shine is already stacked behind the store waiting on you. We wanted to catch them delivering it but we were too late. We have the place under surveillance now and we'll get whoever picks that money up.

"You back in there and load the shine, leave the money and drive back east on route nine. Five mile down the road an unmarked car will follow you home. You stack these cases in your garage until we ask for them.

"You will not take a drink of your cargo. If you do we'll arrest you on new charges you have no immunity on."

Rudy could see no visible sign of surveillance when he backed up to the tarp covered stack of cases behind the market. He grumbled all the time he was loading. Out here at three AM slaving away, loading twenty cases, some of those fellows could have helped him load. He was going to have to unload at home. No one was going to pay him for doing it.

If he had to load it again after this was over they were going to pay him for it. He put the money in the box as directed. He had to stroke it like a pet before he closed the box lid. He remembered the look in Alan's eyes. He put all money in the box slammed the lid and set it down.

The old truck gained speed headed east on route nine. Rudy looked in the rear view mirror and shuddered. He felt sorry for the poor slob who picked the money up.

Two miles down the road his headlights picked something up in the road. It was a couch. Some damned fool hadn't tied it down and it blew out of a pickup. The thing had landed on the center line in a narrow section of the road. It blocked the road. He had to stop and move it.

"That fool should have tied it down." Rudy grunted as he shoved the couch across the lane until his end reached the centerline.

When he turned back toward his truck a man was standing behind him. A closer look in the glow of the headlights revealed the man was wearing a mask. The thing that really caught Rudy's attention was the big twin black holes in the end of the sawed off shotgun pointed at his chest.

"Back into the ditch and lay down." A soft voice commanded.

Rudy complied immediately.

"We'll be back after you later," the voice promised.

Rudy heard the gears scrape and the truck leave but he kept his head down until it was some distance away. When he raised his head he could see the taillights disappearing down a dirt side road.

Rudy rose and walked back to the highway. What should he do? Go west to the waiting chase car or go back to the market and try to contact Alan?

Alan was going to have a fit when he learned Rudy had lost the load of shine.

"OH MY GOD," Rudy screamed when the full impact of what happened hit him. "Alan will never believe me." He groaned to no one in particular. "He'll think I planned this. He'll send me up for twenty years."

The specter of the big black holes in the end of the shotgun whirled back into his mind. He knew why the man didn't pull the trigger and send a swarm of hot lead smashing into his chest, breaking bone, wrecking vital organs and tearing the life from his body. A gunshot would have alerted the revenue agents. He shivered.

Rudy's chest was burning. He staggered to the end of the couch. He rubbed his chest. It was burning even more. Perhaps he should not have eaten that last taco.

What to do now? He had always lived by his wits. He always came up with a way for someone else to pay for his misdeeds. Think!

He rubbed his burning chest again. He could still feel a load of shot ripping it apart.

He sat on the couch. ``What to do? Go to the

chase car? Go back to the market looking for Alan? Either of these was going to get him twenty years. Disappear into the darkness before him?

The urge was strong to leap into the darkness and flee. If he did this Alan and the whole law enforcement world would be looking for him. The image of the man with the shotgun swam back into his mind.

The bootleggers will be looking for him also and his death might not be a sudden smashing of shot. It might be slow and agonizing.

What? Where? His mind searching frantically as he leaned back against the cushion and closed his eyes.

The radio in the unmarked car crackled to life, "That pickup has not passed our position yet." The chase car reported.

Alan looked at his watch and took the microphone down and pushed the transmit button. "He left the market at 3:32 he should have been well past you by now." Alan released the transmit button and thought for a moment. He pressed the button again,

"Chase car proceed this direction. If you meet him proceed on past the market. Do not turn around. Car nine move into the chase car's position and tail the scum bag home when he passes you." Alan hung the microphone back on its hook.

"Do you think Rudy double crossed us?" Bart questioned.

"I don't think so. I don't think he would have the nerve to cross us and why would he give up a free walk for a load of shine?" Alan was puzzled.

"I have found your boy. The truck and the load of shine is no where to be seen. Request your presence on scene now." The radio came to life again.

"What do you mean? No truck and no shine?" Alan squeezed the microphone so hard his knuckles turned white.

"Just that. Do I wait for you or do I begin an investigation?"

"I'll be right there." Alan slammed the microphone back on the hook and jerked the transmission into drive.

"I warned him!" Alan slammed a closed fist on the

steering wheel. "I'll send him so for back in prison they will have shoot beans to him with a cannon."

Sliding the car to a stop Alan leaped from the door and strode toward Rudy on the couch. "I warned you," Alan was pointing a finger and roaring. "I told you ..."

Alan stopped in mid sentence and peered at Rudy. "Rudy?" he questioned.

"He's dead sir." The chase car driver stood nearby. "I haven't been able to ascertain why. I can see no sign of trauma. There is a set of tire tracks on this dirt road. The load of shine must have gone that way." The young officer waited for Alan to digest this information.

"Go down that road and don't lose any time," Alan ordered. Striding back to his car he took the microphone. "All units! Our bird has flown the coop. Move out and block all roads out of here. Detain and search any vehicle capable of carrying twenty cases of shine."

"I found the truck. There is no sign of the bootlegger or the whiskey the truck was hauling."

The chase car reported.

"Get the fingerprint people out. Go over the truck with a fine toothed comb. Alan was so shook up he was issuing orders to everyone and no one.

Bart slapped both hands on the top of the car. "We didn't catch the bootlegger; we lost the load of whiskey. Our stool pigeon is dead. At least we still have the money," he wailed.

Alan and Bart looked at each other. "The money," Alan said. "I sent everyone looking for the truck. No one is watching the money." As one they leaped into the car.

The tires screeched around the market. Their headlight beams hit the back wall. The money box was gone!

Bart began to chuckle. "Perhaps that is the best thing that has happened tonight. All that money was marked and serial numbered. We will get them when they spend it."

Alan laid his head on his hands at the top of the steering wheel. "I don't think so," he said. "The person who pulled this off tonight is smart enough to know the money is marked and serial numbered. He will destroy it. All we're going to catch is flack from the boss for losing the money and ridicule from our cohorts."

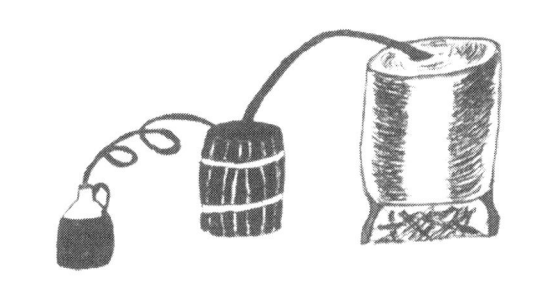

CHAPTER 6

Boredom settled on Vera Lee's shoulders as the lady 4-H speaker droned on. Vera Lee attended this and most local organizational meeting. She had reclaimed her Queen Bee status in the Valley. Now her interests were growing outside of the valley. Local politicians had long since taken notice of this and courted her favor.

Like a school girl, Vera Lee let her attention wander through the window. She watched a butterfly and a hummingbird battle for the nectar a tall flower produced. They danced and twirled through the air like two fairies casting a good spell.

During the past years she had been too busy

working, planning and surviving to see things like this. *I'm going to have to learn to stop and smell the roses,* she thought

In this musing state, Vera Lee's mind drifted to Billy Jack. She wondered what he was doing today. She was amazed at how rapidly he had taken hold of the northern part of her business. The speed at which his business sense and acumen grew and was still growing startled her. He had truly gone from boots to suits. Her feminine intuition told her he was totally devoted to her.

She conjured up his smiling face at the last business dinner they had eaten together. She could still see the little upturn at the corner of his lips when he was amused.

She had been working harder and longer hours with her growing business enterprises than she had worked when she was working as a field hand striving to grow crops in the rocky soil. The returns coming into her bank account were much greater.

"And now a word from Miss Vera Lee Marley, she is one of the major benefactors of this event." The lady stepped away from the microphone.

Vera Lee looked at her watch as she rose. She had to say what she was going to say quickly. She had a meeting with Louis coming up shortly. After that she had a meeting with Robin. When she finished with Robin, Ruby Rail asked for a bit of her time. She looked out over the sea of shining young faces dotted here and there by older troop leader's faces.

Suddenly she felt lonely. She felt something like a personal void in her life. The smiling face of a pretty young girl with curly hair and smile dimples in the front row caught her attention and she wondered what it would be like to have a daughter like this to share the laughter and heartbreaks of life with.

Vera Lee's message was short and to the point. "It is a rapidly changing world. Prepare yourselves to grow and change with it." After speaking a few words she excused herself from the meeting.

Glancing at her watch Vera Lee hurried to the parking lot. Traffic was light and a few minutes later she parked in front of the small building Louis used as an office.

Louis was one of the few disappointments Vera Lee's had suffered lately. Louis did great as long as the fleet consisted of two trucks but when it went beyond that the paperwork ate him up. She spent far too much time checking, correcting, planning and arranging. Louis did a fine job of transporting the shine though. So, she tolerated and helped him,

After the usual greeting Vera Lee seated herself in front of the table Louis used as a desk.

"I sent all my reports in last Friday." Louis leaned back and steepled his fingers.

"I got them. You boys turned a handsome profit last pay period. I'm going to bring in some help for you," Vera Lee watched Louis out of the corner of her eye. "Carl Harper, the fellow purchasing timber for the mill up north doesn't have enough work to keep him busy full time. I'm going to send him down to help you with the paperwork.

"I'm sure you can find something for him to do in the office and it will free you to handle the trucks, maintance, and drivers in the woods." Vera Lee waited for Louis' reaction to this proposal.

Louis sat in silent in thought for a time, "This could work out good. The mill up north is sawing enough lumber it is keeping some of our trucks busy full time. Not to mention the special truck. I hate that pesky paperwork. I'll put Carl in the office for however many hours he can work so I can devote more time to the woods," Louis decided.

"I'm seeing the Highway Patrol and an occasional IRS car looking at fast racy type cars on the highway. I think they are beginning to wonder where the whiskey is coming from. They haven't even glanced at our trucks." Louis waited for Vera Lee's reaction to this bit news.

Vera Lee smiled. She'd accomplished her mission and installed Carl Harper in the office without upsetting Louis. If Carl was good he would be running the logging division of her business in a short time. If Carl wasn't good at the Job she could move him out.

After a short general chat with Louis, Vera Lee headed the Chevy toward home. The sun was above the tree tops but it would be a late supper when she got home. Robin is joining her for supper and Ruby Rail planned to meet with her before bedtime.

Vera Lee wasn't exactly sure what Robin wanted to discus. She'd been a bit cryptic and evasive on the phone. Perhaps she was going to ask for a raise?

During the six months period Vera Lee promised Robin the profit from the bakery, Robin had worked wonders. Robin made more money than she'd ever made before. At the end of the six month period they worked out an equitable wage and Vera Lee let Robin continue to do her thing with the bakery and it continued to grow.

The dirt road into her house was a welcome sight. She thoroughly enjoyed the smell of the forest blowing through the window. The moon was a bright silver ball rising above the top of the trees. The pair of Great Horned Owls were talking softly, planning their nights hunt.

Robin's car was parked at the gate. Vera Lee eased the pickup in beside Robin's car and exited it with a frown on her face. She didn't like for her business associates to converse with her mother. She was not afraid of what her mother might tell them. There was a private and a business side to her life and she liked to keep them separate.

"How did your meetings go dear?" Mother questioned when Vera Lee appeared in the door. Robin sat at the table stirring a bowl of something for mother,

"Very well, hi Robin," Vera Lee hung her purse and keys on their hooks on the wall. "How long until supper?" she asked her mother.

"Another half hour," mother slid a pan onto an unlit burner.

"Come to the office Robin. We'll wait there." Vera Lee led the way.

Vera Lee settled in her chair behind the desk. Robin perched on a chair in front of the desk. Vera Lee leaned back and waited for Robin to open the conversation.

"Did you know the cannery wants to buy the acre of land the bakery is sitting on?" Robin opened.

"I've heard rumors. I haven't had an offer yet." Vera Lee was uncommitted.

"It's true. The Chairman of the Board told me they were expanding and wanted the bakery land." Robin said. "If the bakery sells I'm out of a job."

Vera Lee nodded and waited. Robin didn't come this distance to pass on this information.

"Mister Eisley, owns FARMER'S, it's the first Grocery store I got a sales concession in. Mister Eisley is quite elderly and in bad health. When he passes his heirs will sell the store. I've saved most of the money I've made since going to work for you.

"I don't have near enough to buy the store but I could swing perhaps thirty-five percent. If you could put up sixty-five percent we could become partners and I'd manage the store for my thirty-five percent of the profit." Robin waited for Vera Lee's reaction to the proposal.

Vera Lee remained silent. This was a new idea. She needed time to weigh the pros and cons. She knew she needed the bakery to cover the amount of sugar they were using. The rapid growth of the bakery had covered this issue nicely so far but a grocery store would help.

"We can keep the bakery," It was almost as if Robin read Vera Lee's thoughts. "One side of the store is kind of vacant. With a fairly cheap remodel job we could move the bakery in there.

"This way I would manage the bakery as well as the store.

"I'd like to keep the Granny Whooten club going. Those old ladies are a blast and they are good for business. People purchase stuff from us just to visit and banter with those old ladies. The other day an Internal Revenue Agent had a ball with them. Besides, I know Granny Whooten was mixed up in the bootlegging business when she was young."

"A Revenue Agent was at the bakery?" Vera Lee never blinked or turned a hair.

"Yes," Robin continued, "He didn't show me a badge or anything. He bought a dozen jelly donuts and a thermos of coffee. He looked like he'd been traveling. He sat down, drank a cup of coffee, and ate one of the donuts.

"One of the old Granny Whooten ladies began teasing him about his tie. They all had a good laugh and he moved over to their table.

"All the time they were laughing and joking he was slipping in questions about the bakery." Robin leaned back in her chair.

"I learned to spot Revenue Agents when I was knee high to a gopher. It is funny how them and those generic cars they drive catch your attention." Movement at the door caught Robin's attention.

"Supper is ready!" Mother announced from the door.

"The store sounds like it might be a good proposition. I'll look into it and get back to you." Vera Lee said as she rose from the desk.

"James, Chester James that was the Revenue Agent's name. I remember it from the credit card he used." Snapping her fingers Robin turned toward the kitchen.

One of Dave Maloy's agents! Vera Lee's heart skipped a beat and she was glad Robin's back was turned.

Supper over, Robin on her way, Vera Lee moved in to help mother with the dishes. "You know mother, we could afford to hire someone to help you with the house work."

"Help me?" mother questioned. "Do you mean have some strange woman piddling around in MY house?"

"It wouldn't have to be a stranger. It could be one of the ladies from our church. They could help you clean, cook or whatever." Vera Lee felt the ground going soft under her feet.

"I'm not keeping the house clean enough for you?" Tears rose Mother's eyes.

"You do a wonderful job! I was just thinking of making it easier on you." Vera Lee threw her arms around her mother. Looking out the window over her mother's shoulder she saw headlights approaching the creek crossing.

Ruby Rail met Robin at the creek crossing. Frowning Ruby drove the Mercedes into the six inch deep water flowing down the creek. Ruby did not like driving her car on a dirt road but this account was turning out to be far more lucrative than she thought it would be at the beginning.

The lower floor of the house was awash with light when Ruby approached the yard gate. Taking her briefcase she closed the car door and looked for the flea bitten old hound dog that greeted her last time she was here. She didn't know he'd moved to doggy heaven where the ground was level and the fox were slow.

The owl sent a "Where are you," hoot floating to his mate across the velvety fingers of the night. The wind whispered through the treetops, moving the branches so the moon cast floating, moving shadows everywhere.

'Peace,' thought Ruby. 'Some day I'm going to ditch the city and move to peace.'

"Are you lost?" Vera Lee's voice pulled Ruby out of the trance night had cast over her.

"Lost in the trance of the night," Ruby laughed. "Look at the stars in that sky!"

Vera Lee stepped back as Ruby came through the door. "Go to the office. I will grab us a cup of coffee and be right there."

Ruby looked at her watch when Vera Lee entered

the office. "I will come right to the point. The cannery wants to buy the land the bakery is located on. Here is their offer and I think it is a generous one." Ruby lay a sheaf of papers on the desk.

Ruby settled onto a chair and prepared to wait until Vera Lee was through reading.

After what seemed like a long time to Ruby, Vera Lee laid the papers on the desk. The amount of the offer took her breath away. Pushing the papers toward Ruby she said, "I keep the bakery name and business. I keep the bakery running where it is until I have a suitable building to move it into."

"Do you want me to start looking for a suitable building for the bakery?"

"I have another job for you. I want you to be very discrete and very quiet about this but I want you to find out everything you can about the Farmer's Grocery store."

"Ok, but I haven't heard about it being up for sale or anything." Ruby was puzzled.

"As far as I know it isn't up for sale. I want all the information you can gather quietly." Vera lee repeated. "I want to know who will inherit the store if Mr. Eisley passes away and I want to know all I can about those people. Such as what they do for a living, what their family situation is and what their financial situation is. All you can learn quietly. Do not let them know you are looking at them."

After Ruby's departure Vera Lee dressed for bed and sat in front of her mirror dragging the brush through her hair. The events of the day chased all thoughts of sleep from her head. Thoughts of purchasing the Farmer's store floated through her head.

Taking up her yellow pad she wrote two headings, PROS and CONS on the left and right side of the pages. After a small time she turned the page and wrote FUTURE POSSIBILITIES and then wrote POSSIBLE WAYS and MANNER of purchase.

Moving to the window she listened to the hum of the night forest folks conversing with one another. She listened to the peaceful sounds until her eyelids grew heavy.

Groggily she sat on the side of the bed and rubbed

her face. She needed someone to talk to. Before making a decision of this magnitude she needed all the information she could get.

She thought of driving to the prison and talking to her father. This was something they could talk openly about. The big sticker would be could they trust the discretion of the guard?

The second draw back to this was Jason's limited knowledge. All he knew was limited to the farm and whiskey stills. He'd had no experience in business ventures. If it didn't grow on or was not made on the farm he was at a loss.

Tomorrow she would drive to the pay phone in town and call Billy Jack. Lately his instincts seemed to be right. It never ceased to amaze her how adroitly he'd managed the northern part of her enterprise.

Tossing the hair brush in a drawer she crawled into bed.

What was Chester James, one of Dave's agents, doing at the bakery? Was it an accident? Did the chubby agent wander in to get some donuts or did Dave have his men out sniffing for her trail? Sleep did not come. She stared at a crack in the ceiling.

Back in Nebraska Alan sat drumming his fingers on the files lying on his desk. He cast a jaundiced eye at Bart who sat behind his desk snoring softly. How could the man sleep when they had been made to look like complete fools?

He'd been Bart's partner too long to disturb him. He'd seen Bart snooze, puff and grunt, wipe his face and come up with an idea that solved too many cases. *Nope, let Bart snooze,* Alan thought, *I think better when he's not rambling on about something.*

Moving quietly in order not to disturb Bart, Alan filled his coffee cup. He and Bart lost the bootlegger, the load of bootleg whiskey, the money and their stool pigeon died of a heart attack. They were the laughing stock of the agency. Alan could feel it in his bones. It gnawed and ate him.

No one said anything directly to the fiery tempered Alan. Most had felt the sharp edge of his temper and felt the caustic lashing of his tongue at one time or another. They did however banter the easy going Bart and this drove Alan crazy.

Turning the files one by one Alan went over them again. The agency had arrested several bootleggers selling moonshine but none of them knew where the stuff came from. All the traps and agency efforts had come up empty.

Some of the bootleggers they arrested cooperated with them and left marked or serialized money to pay for the booze. None of the marked money showed up again. The person receiving this money had an uncanny sense of what money was marked. Or, did this person have inside information? Was there a leak in the Internal Revenue Service chain of command? It was a thought that he'd keep in the back of his mind.

Chemical analysis told him that ninety percent of the booze came from the same still. It was good whiskey. That was a good thing. No one was getting killed or blinded by drinking it but there had been no tax paid on it. If the agency could find this still it would put a huge damper on the surge of illegal whiskey on the market.

The pool of arrests for bootlegging had spread

out wider and wider then came back inside again. Alan drew a circle around the arrest areas on the map. He then drew a vertical line from the top of the map to the bottom. After studying the map for a time he drew a horizontal line from the left side to the right side.

The lines crossed on top of the location of his and Bart's office!! Even the map mocked them! Alan slammed the pen into waste basket with such force the rattle woke Bart.

"Umm," Bart rubbed his eyes, "What are you doing?"

"I'm going down in the basement and arrest those bootleggers." Alan rapped on the map with a forefinger. "Look, we're dead center in the middle of this bootlegging ring."

"That's exactly what I've been thinking about," Bart shifted in his chair and rubbed his face. He was still trying to shake the sleep off. "We're looking too close to home. I think that Whiskey Still is somewhere else and the booze is being brought in. Perhaps we should ask for help."

"And who would you ask for help?" Alan was sarcastic.

"We could ask the Revenue Agencies around us to put their ear to the ground so to speak. We could ask them to be alert and check for any suspicious activity in their areas." Bart sat relaxed and watched Alan's face. He knew how this thought was going to be received.

Alan sat silent. His color grew shallow; his nose grew sharp, his lips thinned. His ears seemed to flare out from his head. "After what that bootlegger did to us last time you and I look like damned fools already. Have we got so bad we have to ask someone else to solve our case for us?" Alan paused, "We still have Rudy's partner, Clyde in isolation. He don't know what happened to Rudy. Let's bring him out and squeeze him again. Someone has to know something."

Back at the car dealership Cleo counted the money and set aside the amount going into the bank. He had to admire the little gal. He'd never made this much money in his life. Cleo looked at the ceiling and shuddered; he knew how close he came to dying that night. After her visit to him, he had followed the formula she gave him and it had worked into a very profitable deal.

One time Cleo's curiosity bit him and he put out discrete feelers searching for Vera Lee's identity. He closed the dealership one night and found a scruffy looking fellow leaning on his car. In prison language, the fellow explained to Cleo how much better his health would remain if he ceased this inquiry.

Whoever she was, her double blind system had worked flawlessly up until now. Cleo never knew where or who the booze came from. He was called and told the location he would find the next shipment. He suspected the voice that gave him the location was electronically altered. The message was always short and to the point. There was never time to trace the call.

Randy, Cleo's right hand man, at five feet eight, one hundred fifty pounds was every man on the street. His eyes were brown. His hair was sandy and his manners average. He worked hard to keep his expression mild and placid. His clothing was not good or bad, just average. He dressed and worked hard at being the type of person no one remembered five minutes later.

Behind those mild brown eyes lurked an active, intelligent, well trained brain. Randy was far more intelligent than Cleo but being a little bit lazy he was satisfied with his niche in the bootleg operation.

Randy picked up the booze at a location Cleo gave him and dropped various amounts at locations picked by him. Randy did the work and Cleo handled the money.

If a Bootlegger failed to pay for the whiskey he received the mild mannered Randy became a ruthless enforcer. He handled this in such a manner no one, not even Cleo, knew who the enforcer was but the word on the street said you didn't want to meet him.

It was Randy who master minded taking of the booze and money from Alan and Bart in the Rudy, route nine, fiasco. It had not been for the money he'd taken the chance and retrieved the whiskey and cash. The fiery Alan and laid back Bart had grilled him on a couple of different occasions in the past. He hated them both for being Internal Revenue Agents and he especially hated Alan for his caustic tongue. It gave him great pleasure to make them look like fools. He'd sold the whiskey to another bootlegger and gave Cleo Alan and Bart's marked money.

Cleo knew the money was marked and serial numbered but God bless his greedy little soul he couldn't bring himself to burn that much money. He stashed it away.

He was trying to find a way to pay this marked money to someone he disliked. It had to be done in a manner that couldn't be traced back to him. The opportunity had not presented itself yet but Cleo was positive it would present itself some day and he was sure the feds were still looking for the marked bills.

A burly prison guard pushed Clyde into the interrogation room. He blinked a couple times.

The light was much brighter than the light in his cell block. He looked at himself in the mirror on the wall. The fellow who looked back was not happy. He knew the mirror was really a one way window so people could watch an interrogation without the person being interrogated knowing it. He stuck his tongue out toward the mirror in case someone was observing him now.

It was almost a relief when Alan and Bart walked in. He'd been held in isolation not in the hole. His food and accommodations were much better and his guards were allowed to talk to him but about all he could get out of them was a civil greeting.

There was no telephone, radio, television or communication with the outside world. He'd been supplied with books and been allowed to read but his fifth grade education made reading a chore.

Until now Clyde never realized he could be so hungry for human contact that he'd be glad to see a pair of Internal Revenue agents bringing trouble to him. They could be trouble or his ticket out of this hell hole. It depended on how well he could manipulate them.

"Sit down," Alan ordered as him and Bart entered the room.

"Where is my lawyer?" Clyde demanded. "You're holding me illegally."

"You have not been charged with anything yet so no lawyer has been appointed to defend you. We're holding you on parole violations. You have already had your lawyer on those. If you're in hurry to get to the big house we'll charge you. We have you dead to rights this time."

Alan laid a sheaf of papers on the table and pointed at the chair on the opposite side, "I said sit down! Do I need to call a guard in and handcuff you in that chair?" Alan slapped the table.

Clyde scampered around and sat in the chair. Bart settled his bulk in a chair and placing both elbows on the table, rested his chin on his hands he stared at Clyde. This gave Clyde the hee b jeebys. He imagined all kinds of evil things going on behind that sleepy gaze.

Alan slid into a chair and leaned forward. "We

need the name of the operator and location of the whiskey still you were hauling the whiskey for."

Clyde opened his mouth and closed it.

"We want the truth. Don't be thinking up lies." Alan slapped the table openhanded again.

"Like I told you before, I don't know where or who. I was just killing time when Rudy … Wait a minute! Where is Rudy? What have you done with Rudy?" Clyde sat up straight.

Alan and Bart exchanged glances. "Rudy's dead." Bart spoke for the first time.

"You killed Rudy! You killed Rudy!" Clyde screamed.

"No, we did not kill Rudy!" Alan said. "We think your buddy, the whiskey maker, did it." Alan lied easily. "Rudy had a load of whiskey out on route nine. Someone robbed him. He was dead and the whiskey was missing when we found him."

"Rudy dead?" Clyde settled back with a sob.

"We were hoping you could help us catch Rudy's killer." Bart said softly.

"Like I told you before, I was soaking up some

rays on the corner of the school ground and Rudy came and asked me to help him move some whiskey. I thought we were going to get a bottle to drink. I didn't know we were picking up a load to peddle." Clyde could lie also.

"You give us the name of that bootlegger and we'll get Rudy's killer and let you out." Alan waited.

"You guys are grasping at straws. You have nothing or you wouldn't be here talking to me. You sure wouldn't be offering me deals. Is Rudy really dead or are you trying to trick information out of me?" Clyde had quieted enough to think.

"Rudy is definitely dead. We need information and you need a friend. You're looking at a bunch of rough years." Alan was trying to keep it low key.

Clyde sat silent. His Jaw locked. *Could Rudy really be dead?* He asked himself.

"We're going to move you to the general population in the jail. If you hear anything about the snatching of the whiskey that killed Rudy let us know. I know some fool is going to brag about it." Alan gathered the sheaf of papers. "They always do."

"You let me out of here and I'll find the man that killed Rudy." Clyde said softly.

"I'll tell you what we're going to do," Alan shuffled the papers and tapped the edges on the tabletop to square them up, "We're going to put you in with the general population and leave you there for now.

"If you are smart and listen more than you talk you might get some information that would be useful to us. If so we will help you with your sentence. We'll find the guy who robbed and killed Rudy."

"I want out. You've held me longer than legal without a hearing or bail." Clyde tried again.

"Ok, if you want to do that we'll charge you. Again, we're holding you on parole violations. We will add the possession of whiskey the taxes have not been paid on with the intent to sell. We'll talk to the DA and you will be on your way to the big house for many long years. With the parole violations you will get no bail. They'll just bring you back from prison to stand trial for the whiskey violations."

"We can't help you once these charges have been filed. It's out of our hands." Alan's lips thinned and his gaze bore into Clyde. "What will it be? Do you want to help us or take a long vacation behind bars?"

"Ok, Ok!! I'll take the jail time. I want the man who killed Rudy." Clyde leaned forward and laid his head on the table.

After the deputy removed Clyde Alan and Bart sat in silence.

"I think we should try another stake out with a stool pigeon. We have enough of them now. We can get one to cooperate." Alan ventured.

"This bootlegger is pretty wily. What can we do different this time?" Bart was skeptical.

'Well, for one thing we'll seal the place off until our man can't escape with the money. We'll block all roads out of the place and have plenty of men in place to grab him. Another Rudy caper would be too much." Alan shuddered.

CHAPTER 7

The phone rang three times before Billy Jack answered. "Good morning."

"I was hoping to catch you before you went to work. I need some advice." Vera Lee's voice had a lilt in it.

"All right I'll give you advice. Get rid of all the junk and move up here." Billy Jack advised with a chuckle.

"You would regret that in short order." Vera Lee laughed. "But seriously a situation has arisen. I've been made an offer and I'd like your take on it."

Billy Jack listened attentively while Vera Lee explained the situation to him.

"It sounds like it could be a deal. I've been keeping an eye on Robin. She is an up and coming person." Billy Jack said. "She most likely could manage the store and keep it profitable."

"Do you know Robin?" Vera Lee demanded. "Have you met her?"

"I met her a long time ago. Back in the good old days I used to run a load of shine for her daddy occasionally. She was just a young girl then. I haven't seen her in person since those days. When you made the bakery deal with her I began checking up on her."

Vera lee was silent for a moment. The stir of jealousy was a strange feeling she had not felt for some time. "You never told me you knew Robin." She accused.

"You never asked and it never has been important. There are very few people you deal with I don't watch." Billy Jack was matter of fact. "I'll think about this and get back to you. One thing I'm sure of. You'll need a lawyer to safeguard you and handle the legal end of it. I don't think I'd want one of the old established law firms dabbling in my business. There is a new law firm in Medlock. I'd check with them if I were you."

"OK," Vera Lee was subdued. Billy Jack knew Robin? Billy Jack knew Medlock, Texas well enough to know a new law firm had moved in. How well did Billy Jack know Robin?

Vera Lee hung up the phone and waved at Freddy Mantiss one of two local policemen who patrolled the short streets of the small town. Freddy wheeled the police car into the curb.

"Hey, beautiful," he greeted Vera Lee.

Vera Lee answered with a wave and a smile.

"There's a dance at the Elks Club over in the county seat Saturday. How about going over with me?"

"I'm going to be busy. I have business out of town this weekend." Vera Lee lied. Then she decided it wasn't a lie. She was going to see Billy Jack to discuss the impending purchase of the market. She lied to herself.

She stood watching the receding patrol car until

it disappeared around the corner. *If I could have stood a man with a badge pinned to his shirt I would have been married long ago,* she thought.

"Get going," She told herself, "You have to let mom know where you are going and pack."

After spending a fun filled and informative weekend with Billy Jack in Nebraska Vera Lee wheeled the pickup into a parking lot in Medlock, Texas. The sun was shining but Jack Frost had bit the head off all the flowers in the box she parked beside. Golden leaves blew across the black pavement. The gold lettering on the door proclaimed J. D. Wheeler Attorney At Law.

At the tinkle of the bell on the door the young attorney behind the desk looked up. At the sight of the attractive young lady entering the room J.D. automatically straightened his tie and rose from the desk. His lively blue eyes swept the lady from shoes to face. His right hand swiped the close cropped sandy hair. Both hands dropped to tug at the bottom of the immaculate suit coat. "Could I help you?" He found his voice.

"Do you practice corporate law?" Vera Lee came right to the point.

"Please be seated," J.D. held the chair. "I do handle corporate law. What can I do for you?"

"Is everything I tell you held in strict confidence?" Vera Lee noted the lawyer's height was about four inches greater than her own. There was real suppleness in the broad shoulders and arms.

"Yes mam. Everything that is said here stays here." J.D. assured her. "I'm J.D. wheeler. What can I do for you?"

"I'm Vera Lee Marley. Do you deal in the sale of property and partnership contracts?" Vera Lee stayed with the point.

"Those are my specialty. What do you need?" J.D. settled behind his desk.

"I want to buy the Farmer's Market grocery store and I want to set up a partnership to purchase and run it." Vera Lee watched J.D.'s face. He did show some surprise.

"I didn't know it was for sale." J.D. searched his mind.

"It is not for sale right now but Mr. Eisley is in bad health and won't live long. There are two sets of heirs. No one knows which one the old gentleman is going to leave the store to. He may split it between them. It doesn't matter to me.

"What I propose to do is to go to each of those possible heirs and offer them $1,000.00 for an option on the store for a specified amount of money if they inherit it. This way I can avoid a bidding war with other companies or individuals when the time comes. I believe the heirs will go along with this because they get the thousand dollars even if they don't inherit the store. Can you handle things like this?" Vera Lee leaned back and let J.D. think.

J. D. leaned back in his chair, examined his finger nails, and looked at the ceiling. Wow! This lady was not only good looking she had the power to look and plan ahead. She must have some money also. She was a lady after his own heart. He wanted to know more about her and this situation.

"Look at the clock. It is lunch time and I'm hungry. Would you go to lunch with me? There's a restaurant down the street with private tables. We can talk in confidence. No one can over hear us. You explain the whole deal to me and I'll tell you what I can do. I'm buying the lunch. You can't get a better deal than that," J.D. smiled when she hesitated.

There were several empty tables when they entered the restaurant. The waitress ushered them to a table near a window in the back corner. It was sufficiently secluded that normal conversation couldn't be overheard.

The food was good and J.D. kept her laughing. Vera Lee decided he must be a good lawyer from the subtle way he wove questions as to her marital and current boyfriend status into the business conversation.

She paid J.D. a retainer fee to represent her. His job was to work out the contracts, form a legal partnership with Robin and attend to the legal angles of purchasing the Farmer's Market.

J.D. left with a smile on his face. He had a large check in his pocket as a retainer fee and he was going to see that it took a lot of consultation and perhaps several dinners to get all this work accomplished.

Leaving J.D's office Vera Lee squared the truck in the road. With the truck gaining speed she settled back to think. It had been a pleasant lunch as well as getting some of the things that had been bugging her accomplished.

Besides working out some of her problems she had thoroughly enjoyed the lunch. J.D. had a great smile, a good sense of humor and he kept her laughing all through it.

What would Daddy think of his little girl now? Time was passing. How was she going to work him into her operation when he was released from prison? Would his prison time cure him of the temper outbursts? Questions swirled in her mind.

Vera Lee watched a big truck fly past her. What would mother think if she knew she was buying a big grocery store? Vera Lee had her mother's power of attorney so she could run the whole thing through in the name of Ruth Stiller. Mother would be flabbergasted if she knew how much money had been made and spent in her name last year.

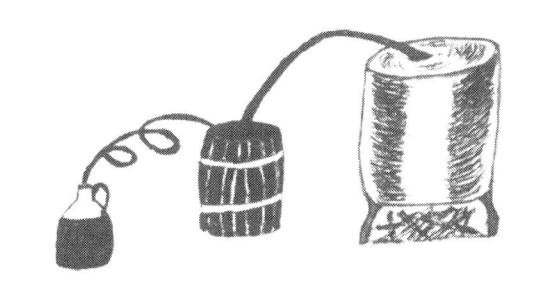

CHAPTER 8

The drop point was pretty much as usual. It was a closed business with fairly poor lighting but with a wide driveway and large parking lot.

The ten cases of shine were stacked against the wall as promised. The money box sat in the promised place.

"There will be no slip ups this time!" Alan adamantly demanded of the group of policemen pressed into service for this sting. "We're not going to use the stool pigeon to pick the booze up. We'll use an agent of the same size and build. He will be wearing the stool pigeon's clothes. When the bootlegger comes for the money box we'll get him."

"The Highway Patrol is working with us this time. Every road, highway and dirt pig trail out of here will be closed when I give the signal. It was good you thought of bringing in the K-9 teams." Alan nodded to a uniformed policeman.

"If the fellow leaps from a vehicle and runs into the night he will be easier to catch." Bart was building more faith in the operation.

"What gripes me is that we had to offer this slime ball Pigeon the same deal we gave Rudy to get his cooperation." Alan gripped. "Oh well, we're using a minnow to catch a shark."

The agents moved into hiding. Alan didn't think there would be any action until later but he wanted everyone in place and prepared for whatever happened. Along with his hatred he had a profound respect for the bootlegger's ability. Each and every one of the officers involved knew what happened last time a stakeout was set up for this bootlegger.

None of them wanted to be the butt of the jokes that had past around the station house after the last fiasco. Two thirds of the officers present had managed to crack at least one joke at Alan and Bart's expense. Now the dime was on their back. None wanted the sharp lashing Alan's tongue was capable of delivering either. Even the Academy trainees remained at a high level of alert.

As expected the earlier part of the night passed uneventfully.

At ten o'clock the agent disguised as the bootlegger drove the bootlegger's pickup in and after looking the place over for cameras he loaded the shine stacked against the wall, put the money in the box and drove out.

The hours dragged on. Bart's toes began to itch. The ground he lay on got harder and the small sticks began to gouge into his soft flesh. He tried to rub his shoes together to solve some of the itch problem.

"Stop it!" Alan whispered "Stop rubbing and squirming! Your movement will be spotted and you're making enough noise to wake the dead."

Hour after hour they watched. Bart drifted off

into sleep. Alan scowled at him but decided to let him sleep. He was being still and a lot quieter asleep than he was when he was awake. Alan also knew Bart woke up instantly. He didn't need to go through the eye rubbing and stretching stuff. He was ready for action instantly.

Gray fingers were pushing their way over the eastern horizon when Alan poked Bart in the ribs. "There's something moving on the road out front," he whispered into Bart's ear. It is going on past. No, it's coming in it must be our man. Get ready with that light switch but don't turn it on until I tell you."

They could see movement between the shadows the trees cast across the driveway. Slowly it worked its way up the driveway. It seemed like a lifetime to Bart whose skin had seemed to absorb the sticks and pebbles of the uneven ground. His leg'd gone to sleep and his toes itched twice as much. All this and he didn't dare move a muscle. Alan would kill him.

The movement stopped at the corner of the building. After a pause it came around the corner and stopped in the feeble glow of the pole light. It was a dog! A German shepherd type dog! The dog raised its head and tested the air.

Bart gathered himself to shift his bulk to a more comfortable position.

Alan sensed the coming movement and whispered. "Don't move. There's most likely someone coming in behind the dog. The dog's not acting like a stray. It's listening and smelling. I suspect the slime ball has trained a dog to come in and look for traps."

The dog moved to the money box and took the handle in his mouth. Lifting the money box the dog trotted toward the corner.

It took Alan a moment to realize what was happening. The dog was leaving with the money box! "Turn the light on!" Alan bellowed. Leaping to his feet, he drew his service weapon on the way up.

It took the startled Bart a moment to react and turn the lights on. At the same time the lights came on Alan's first shot dug a small furrow in the pavement near the dog's feet and whined off into the night.

Stung by the fragments of pavement the bullet sprayed around, the startled dog who decided he wasn't welcome and leaped away at full speed.

"Kill him! Kill him!" Alan bellowed as he sent shot after shot in the dog's direction.

The other agents were not positioned to see the dog pick up the money box. They were looking for a human to shoot and could find none. The dog streaked across the road and disappeared into a field overgrown with brush and tall grass.

"Bring the dogs in. Bring the dogs in." Alan shouted into the hand held radio and ran to the spot where the dog disappeared. Not again, he couldn't have been made a monkey of again. The last round had been bad. This time it will be twice as bad.

"Turn your dog loose and let him catch that German Shepherd!" Alan bellowed at the first K9 unit to arrive.

"Dog? Did you say dog?" the K9 officer was confused.

"Yes, a German Shepherd carrying the money box. Send him into that field and catch the dog. Do it now!" Beside himself, Alan ordered again as the second K9 unit rolled in.

"Hold up minute," Bart took the K9 Officer by the arms and explained what had happened.

"Our dogs are not trained to trail other dogs. Our dogs are trained to trail people. We will send them into the field. If there was a human in the field with the dog we'll get him but our dogs will not bother the German shepherd. They are strictly trained to ignore other dogs."

"Don't stand there talking! Get into that field and bring that money box back." Alan ordered.

"There is a possibility the dog dropped the box. Check the field as thoroughly as possible. I will have a group out to search in a few hours." Bart's feeling of impending disaster had come to pass.

Alan stomped over and sat behind the steering wheel of the K9 car and watched the K9 group search the field. Laying his head on the steering wheel he pounded the dash with both hands. "Not again," he yelled.

A mile and a half away, on top of a small hill,

Randy took the money box from the dog's mouth. "Good boy Shep!" he praised and petted the dog. "You did exactly as you were trained to do. Things got a little rough down there did they? I heard the gunfire." Randy placed a hand on either side of Shep's head and shook it side to side with his fingers digging into the ruff around his neck, while doing this Randy checked Shep for any kind of injury. Shep loved this kind of play.

"I'm afraid you worked yourself out of a job this time. They will be waiting for you with a net or rifles next time." Randy carefully opened the money box and shook his head. All that beautiful money had been marked and serialized. It was totally worthless now. He thought about giving it to Cleo but decided to have some fun with it instead. He thought of this project after he gave the marked money to Cleo last time. Another idea was floating in the back of his head. He took a few of the bills and folded them into his shirt pocket.

Three days later an excited Alan burst into the IRS office. "Come on Bart! Some of the marked money has shown up. The first National Bank called. They have some of the marked money. Let's get on the trail. I want that slime ball so bad I can taste it. I'm going to crush him. I'm going to grind him under my heel." This was the happiest Bart had ever seen the sober sided Alan be.

Alan weaved through the city traffic. "We'll trail this money right back to that bootlegger and I'll see he gets twenty years for the trouble he has caused," Alan swore. "We may have to track it back through the stores but we'll get him. Wait until I get my hands on him!"

"If we get him pretty soon he will still have some of the money with him and then we'll have the goods on him for sure." Bart was enjoying watching the exuberant Alan.

Slamming the car into a handicapped parking place they raced up to the bank President's office.

The pretty secretary smiled at them. "The President has visitors in his office but he said send you in as soon as you got here." She pointed at a door with a lot of gold lettering on it.

Alan was three steps ahead of Bart when he burst through the door. There was the usual big desk with the President occupying the chair behind the desk. A man sat at the end of the desk. He was an older man with white hair and a kindly smile on his lips. He was also dressed in the full garb of a Catholic Priest. Over by the wall two Nuns perched on hard chairs.

"Um, we need to talk to you about police business." Alan came to a screeching halt and cast a knowing eye from the bank President to the Padre.

"Yes, I know," the bank President steepled his hands on his desk. "You want to talk to me about the marked money we received. Well, since Father Sheethy and the sisters deposited the marked money. I thought you might want to talk to them also."

"How did they get their hands on it?" Alan demanded. He was having trouble slowing down.

"I don't know, have a seat and we'll discuss it." The President motioned toward an empty chair.

"How did you get the money, Father?" Bart

interceded, smiling at Alan and nodding at the Priest.

"Our widows and orphan funds are pitifully low. We cannot meet our present obligations. We started a drive to raise funds for this worthy cause. We put a box in front of the alter. At the last mass father Xavier requested our parishioners to donate money to support this worthwhile charity.

"We thought our prayers had been answered until Mr. Baxter called us and said the money had been stolen or something of that sort." Father Sheethy leaned back in the chair and waited.

"Do you know which of your people donated this money?" Alan asked eagerly.

"No, we left the box near the alter. Our church is never locked. It is open twenty four hours a day seven days a week. People can come and pray anytime they feel the need. This money was dropped in the box during the night. We have a Priest on duty all night but I'm afraid he dozes off sometimes. We were so thrilled." Father Sheethy finished lamely.

"How much money was in the box?" Bart asked.

"Um," Mr. Baxter cleared his throat. "Nearly all the money you had us looking for is here. It was in the deposit Father Sheethy and the Sisters just made. There are a few dollars missing."

Alan seemed to shrink in his chair. His open hand came down on Baxter's desk with a resounding smack. "He's playing games with us!" He roared. "This bootlegger is laughing at us."

Mr. Baxter leaned backward so sharply his chair rolled away from the desk. The Nuns leaped to their feet. Even Bart flinched. The only person unmoved was Father Sheethy.

"Now, now," Bart soothed. "It's not all that bad. We got the money back. That will make the boss happy."

"Must you take all the money back?" Father Sheethy leaned forward. "The mothers and wee one need it desperately. Couldn't a part of it be donated?"

"Father, that money does not belong to us. It belongs to the feds. We must return it to our boss. All of it." Alan leaned forward and put his face in his hands. Rising he held both hands out toward Bart, "This bootlegger has us, me and you, starving widows and orphans now."

Silence engulfed the room. Bart took his wallet from its resting place. Taking all the bills from the wallet he tossed them on the table in front of the Priest and looked pointedly at Alan.

Alan shook his head, snorted and then reached for his billfold. Removing all the folding money he hesitated, lifted a concealed flap and added another hundred dollar bill to those bills in his hand. With a blood red face he tossed the money in front of the priest stalked from the room.

"That is the best we can do for you father," Bart said on his way to the door.

Alan was silent and morose after leaving the bank. Weaving through the city traffic he slid the car into his reserved parking spot at the Federal Building. Slamming the door he stalked off in the direction of the stairwell.

Bart retrieved the bag containing the marked money and turned toward the elevators. He wasn't as upset as Alan. After all, they had retrieved almost all the money. They were making some progress and sooner or later this bootlegger was going to slip up. All they needed was one slipup on the bootlegger's part and it was all over. The fat lady would sing and they could go back to his favorite pastime of being bored.

When Bart entered the squad room Alan sat brooding at his desk. "I know we've been through this before but let's do it again. It takes; heat, sugar, grain, yeast and water, to make 'shine." Alan ticked each item off on his fingers.

"The heat can come from any source; wood, coal, natural gas, propane, oil or electricity.

"The sugar can come from: any form of refined sugar, molasses, sugar cane, honey or most anything sweet.

"Alcoholic beverages can be made from most any kind of grain but from our analysis we know this still is using corn.

"The yeast could be a home brewed or commercial variety.

"There are thousands of rivers, springs, wells, and water companies out there to supply the water."

Alan paused to look at Bart. Bart's head was hanging to one side in his after noon nap. Alan slid the top drawer of his desk open and pulled a water pistol out of it. Moving to the water fountain he turned it on and let it run until it reached maximum cold. He then filled the water pistol. Checking to make sure the pistol was completely full of water he pointed it at a trash can and pumped the trigger until he had a good stream going.

Taking careful aim at Bart's head Alan pumped the trigger vigorously.

"Whaa!" Bart leaped from the chair, knocking it over backward behind him.

"Wakeup!" Alan was chuckling, "we have a bootlegger to catch."

"I was sitting there thinking about that," Bart wiped as much of the water as possible off the front of his shirt. He glared at Alan for a moment then smiled. "It was worth it to see you grin. You sober sided son a slow flying seagull. What I was thinking was that last time I took the sugar and grain investigation and you took the rest. This time you take the sugar and grain end. Maybe one of us will come up with something worthwhile.

"The only thing I found last time was a bakery in Medlock, Texas using an increased amount of sugar and yeast. I called an agent down south, Chester James, and had him drop by and look it over.

"Chester said the bakery had sold and a new manager took over. The new manager was a go getter. She has begun supplying baked goods to grocery stores and other outlets. The business is expanding at a rapid rate. The increased amount sales could explain the increased sugar use. He said something else, something funny, and something about a Granny Whooten Donut Club."

"I'll take another look at the sugar and the grain." Alan raised the water pistol.

Bart pointed a finger at him. "You better put that thing back in your desk and forget which drawer it is in. I still think we should call on the neighboring agencies to help us with this case."

"No, keep the faith baby. We will solve it. I owe this bootlegger. I'm tired of getting laughed at," Alan was positive. "The bootlegger has made us look like monkeys. Everyone is laughing at us. I want him. If we keep picking at it we'll get him. There is still a small amount of that marked money out there. Maybe he'll mess up and spend It.

CHAPTER 9

Vera Lee parked in front of the bakery and watched a truck loaded with tomatoes slow, make a wide swing, and enter the cannery. She checked her watch. It was the time Robin was supposed be here. JD setup a meeting with Mr. Eisley's likely heirs. As a working partner Vera Lee wanted Robin present at the meeting.

Vera Lee wondered exactly how much Robin was connected with Billy Jack. Robin was a vivacious, good looking, hard working woman who was going somewhere. This would be the type of woman who could catch Billy Jack's attention. This question had rattled around inside her head ever since Billy Jack told her he'd been checking on Robin.

Of course Billy Jack was a man on his way up. He was handsome and fun to be with. Robin was sure to be attracted to him. Billy Jack told her he'd been checking all the people she was doing business with. Did this mean he was interested in Robin? Or did it mean he just a loyal employee looking out for his job? What were her feelings for Billy Jack? Was he just a good friend? If her feelings were more than friendship why did she feel so strongly attracted to JD? She thought less often of David Maloy. Everything was getting all muddied up.

"Sorry I'm late." Robin swung the right door open and leaped in. "There were some last minute orders and I had to pitch in and help fill them. Didn't you say we had a meeting with the heirs to the Farmers Market?"

Vera Lee twisted the key and the faithful Chevrolet roared. "JD has worked up some definite proposals. Open the glove box and read the last minute changes in the proposal. There are only a couple of things I suggested. That will be the only variation to the copy I sent for you to study."

"I took my copy down to the yellow Rose and went over it very thoroughly while I ate dinner. You and JD did a complete job. I couldn't think of anything else to add." Robin waved a hand at a man standing on the curb.

"Was that your boyfriend?" Vera Lee asked.

"No, that is the manager of Sheffield Grocery. We supply their store with baked goods. I don't have time for a boyfriend now and if we get Farmer's Market I'll have even less time." Robin leaned back against the cushion enjoying the moment's relaxation.

"It seems like a lifetime since we first had dinner at the Yellow Rose." Vera Lee shook her head.

"You know, to me it don't seem that long. I was dying when I worked for Uncle Joe. Every day drag on forever. After you bought the place and promoted me I have spent every waking hour planning or working. If I wasn't actually working I was planning and visiting other establishments trying to sell our products or get new ideas for our products.

Time has sort of slid away from me. "I do

appreciate what you done for me." Robin closed her eyes. "If you had not come along and gave me a chance I'd probably be slinging hash at the Yellow Rose today."

"You earned all you've gotten. I can't see you slinging hash very long. Here we are." Four cars were parked in front of JD's office. I'd guess our heirs are all here." Vera Lee expertly slid the pickup into a parking place.

"Here, will you carry this," Vera lee handed a fat bank bag to Robin.

Gathering up their purses and a hand full of papers they headed for the door marked J.D. Wheeler Attorney at law.

J.D. was sitting in the conference room where he could see the front door. When Vera Lee and Robin stepped through the door he rose and motioned for them to come back.

"Sit over there J. D.," pointed at a table. A man sat at the end of the table and man and woman sat about the middle of the table. "This is Henry Eisley, and this is Walter and Alma Bingham. Henry is Mister Eisley's son and Alma is Mister Eisley's daughter. Turning J. D. extended a hand toward Vera Lee and robin. "This is Vera Lee Marley and Robin Kowlowsky. They are the ladies who wish to make you an offer." J.D. sat back in his chair. "I took the liberty of providing Henry and the Binghams with a copy of your offer. They are aware of your proposal."

Alma screwed up her face and said, "We weren't going to come to this meeting. But, we decided that we should attend any meeting that has anything to do with our inheritance." Alma sent a withering glance at Henry.

Vera Lee very deliberately spread the paper work in hand on the table. Then, pulling the chair back she pulled her hackles in and sat down. Robin plopped in the chair beside her.

"As you know we are making you an offer for an option on the Farmers Market. Should you inherit the market we will buy it at the sum written in the option you sign. We will pay each family a thousand dollars for this option. The thousand dollars is yours to keep. If you don't inherit the market you keep the money. If you inherit the market we buy it. If ..."

"What if we inherit it and get a higher offer for the place?" Walter interrupted.

"That is an unlikely thing. If you read the proposal carefully you will see that we've had three financial institutions appraise the store. Their appraisals were remarkably close to each other. You will notice that we averaged all the appraisals and dropped the price by a thousand dollars. If you inherit the store your thousand dollars will go into the purchase price. If you don't inherit the market you will have a thousand dollars that you would not have had and can spend for anything you want.

"You will have gotten something out of the store. As it is, if you don't inherit the store you will get nothing." Vera Lee paused to let this sink in.

"If you accept our thousand dollars and sign the option it is a legal and binding document. If you inherit the store you will sell the store to us as agreed." Vera Lee looked at J. D. who nodded his head in the affirmative.

"I'm going to have to think about this offer," Walter said. "Perhaps we should get two thousand dollars."

"No, the thousand dollars represents over six month's wages for the common labor today. We don't negotiate any higher or lower. One thousand it is." Vera Lee was firm. "This is a thousand dollars you will be getting for free if you don't inherit."

"I'll take the thousand dollars," Henry leaned forward and put both hands on the table. "I can see the value of the proposal."

Alma looked at Henry like he had made her eat a prune.

"Ok," Vera Lee opened the bank bag and removed two huge stacks of five dollar bills. They were banded twenty bills in a bundle. Ten bundles were banded into each stack. Each stack contained two hundred five dollar bills. She sat one stack beside her elbow and the other between her and Henry. "Of course Mister Wheeler here will take care of the signing of the option and get a recipe for the money." She nodded toward J.D.

Alma gasped as if she had been struck when Vera Lee pulled the bundles of bills from the bank bag. She couldn't take her eyes off it.

Vera Lee pretended to ignore the Binghams and turned her shoulder to them like she was concentrating on Henry and J. D. In reality she was enjoying Alma's reaction to the stack of bills. When she turned her elbow knocked the stack of bills over and pushed them a bit.

"Honey, that would remodel my kitchen and …" Alma was trying to talk quietly out the side of her mouth to Walter.

"Yes, or buy me an automobile. Miss Maloy," Walter raised his voice, "We will sign that option for fifteen hundred dollars." Walter had to try again.

Vera Lee never turned. "No," she said. "One thousand dollars was what I had in mind. I guess I'll just take that thousand and buy me another truck. Mine is getting old." Vera Lee's elbow bumped the stack of bills and turned them again.

What was with this lady? Walter wondered. She isn't going to budge. He looked at Alma; she was vigorously nodding her head in the affirmative.

"I guess we'll sign for the thousand," Walter gave in grudgingly.

The paper work was all signed and the copies were resting safely in Vera Lee's purse. The potential heirs had departed the premises.

"Whoo wee" J.D. said. "Where did you get the Idea for that stack of bills? It set me back as much as it did Miss Alma. I about chocked when you pulled those stacks of bills out. We have to celebrate this. How about I buy you dinner?" J.D. asked Vera Lee.

"No," Vera Lee shook her head. "Robin rode up with me I have to get her back."

"How about if I buy both of you dinner?" J.D. persisted.

Vera Lee looked at Robin who nodded. "You are on and I'm hungry enough to eat a whole cow." Meanwhile, Cleo sat behind his desk so he could see the yard out of the plate glass window. He'd been sitting here for some time drumming his fingers on the desk and watching the lot. A shipment of shine had been delivered and Randy was late with the payment. Cleo wanted his greedy, pudgy little fingers on the money. He loved the feel of it.

Cleo couldn't believe Randy would try to keep the money for himself. The Randy Cleo knew was the easygoing nondescript person Randy worked hard at projecting to other people. He'd never seen Randy the collector who punished a bootlegger that tried to not pay for the product delivered. He had no idea of the avarice that lived in Randy's soul.

Cleo was relieved and agitated when he saw Randy turning in from the street. It was about time! He watched Randy park near the door and saunter into the office.

"It's about time you got here. Where have you been? Where is the money from the last delivery?" Cleo's demands came quickly to the point.

Randy stopped to stare at Cleo, "Hello Randy, come in and have a seat. How are things going with you? It is good to see you again." Randy's voice grew more insolent as he went along. Grabbing a chair beside Cleo's desk he spun it around, straddled it, and sat facing Cleo.

Cleo turned red and stared back, "Well, where is the money?" he demanded.

"What money?"

"You know what money," Cleo bellowed and slapped his desk. "The feds turned another bootlegger against us. They were laying in wait again. The money was serial numbered and marked." Randy paused.

"How do you know?" Cleo asked.

"Man," Randy turned his head and stared out the door for a few seconds. "The Feds were there in force. They had half of the state and county police patrolling the roads in that area. Had a man retrieved the money box he couldn't have drove, walked or flew out of there without getting caught. They fired several shots at Shep when he picked up the money box.

"Do you think they would go to all that trouble and leave clean money in the box?" Randy held both hands up and waited for an answer.

"Do you expect me to believe all that? Where is the money?" Cleo demanded once more.

"I gave it to the widows and orphan's fund at the Catholic Church." Randy smiled at the memory.

"You what? That was my money!" Cleo roared. "I ordered you to bring it to me."

"That money was worthless to us. We couldn't spend it. It was marked. They are waiting for us to spend a dollar of it." A grain of suspicion began working its way into Randy's brain. "Where is the last batch of marked money I brought you? Did you find a way to laundry or fence that money? If you did I want my cut of it."

"Do you think the people at the church won't tell the Feds where they got the money?" Cleo asked.

"They don't know how they got the money. I put it in a collection box near the Alter. There was no one around." Randy smiled again. "I would like to have been there and saw their face when the Feds busted out to arrest the people who spent that money and found themselves robbing a bunch of widows and orphans."

Randy shifted gears and the smile vanished from his face. "If you sold the last batch of marked money

I want my share of it, now!" It was Randy's turn to demand.

"The money is in my safe over there. I'll let you know if I find a way to fence it. You will get your share." Cleo nodded his head. He was feeling the ground go mushy under his feet. It was time to get the subject off the last batch of money. "You will do what I tell you and bring all the money to me."

"I thought we went into this as partners. That was the deal we made when you needed my customers to sell your moonshine to.

You were to handle the money and I'd handle the delivery. We split the profit fifty-fifty." Randy waited for an answer.

"That's what I'm telling you. I handle the money. From this day forward you will do as I say and bring me the money." Cleo was feeling better now. "I need the marked money so I can prove to the still operators that we're being honest with them.

"I have some stuff I have to do now." Cleo shifted gears. "We will continue this discussion later. I have to pay the county a permit fee for a license to run this dump. The money and paperwork is laying on my desk. Will you run it down to the Court House and pay it for me?"

Randy was on the verge of saying he wasn't an errand boy when he noticed the extra telephone on Cleo's desk beside the paperwork. *Of course,* He thought, *that's the way he knows where the whiskey is dropped. They phone him.*

Placing himself between Cleo and the desk he picked up the money, the paperwork and memorized the number written in the center of the dial on the second phone. Without a word he walked out.

Cleo breathed a sigh of relief. For a moment he thought there was going to be serious trouble.

Randy drove to the edge of the lot, pulled a pad out of the glove compartment and wrote the phone number he had memorized.

I'm not an errand boy. I'm a full partner. I will not be treated this way. Cleo has got too big for his britches. I'll bet he's managed to sell the marked money and is holding out on me. Randy growled to himself. *I'll know very soon if that money is still in the safe.*

Pulling his billfold from his pocket he removed the small amount of marked money he'd kept when he visited the Catholic Church. Taking a like amount from the money Cleo sent to pay the permit fees he placed the marked money on top of the pile, snapped the rubber band back into place, tossed the money back on the seat and headed for the county offices whistling.

Randy rented a small apartment on the top floor of an apartment complex. From the single outside window he could look down the street and see Cleo's car lot.

Bart leaned back at his desk. He was wide awake and drumming his fingers. Alan was uncharacteristically late this morning.

"Good morning sleeping beauty," Bart said when Alan strode across the floor and plopped into his chair.

"I had some stuff to check on this morning. I was out working while you were curled up snoozing. You never seem to catch up on your sleep so I didn't bother you." Alan's demeanor told Bart that what ever he was checking on didn't work out well.

A smile worked its way across Bart's face. "The bank called a little while ago. They have the rest of our money. It came in last nights deposits."

Alan sat up right and leaned on his desk. "Where did it come from?"

"It came from the county this time. The bank is holding it for us." Bart started to rise.

"Hang on here a minute!" Alan held a hand up. "What is that bootlegger up to this time? He has made a fool of us every time. Let's think about this. The county ... the county, how could he use the county to stick us? I'm tired of looking bad and that widows and orphans thing got me. I'm not about to put out another hundred and fifty dollars."

"I'm glad I didn't have a hundred fifty dollars." Bart pushed his chair away from his desk. "Come on, we'll go see what the bootlegger has in store for us. He is going to slip and then it is our turn."

Alan wheeled the car into a handicap parking place near the bank. And they climbed the stairs to the bank president's office.

"I'm going to have to give you a ticket for parking there," Bart said between puffs. You supposed to be setting an example for the citizenry."

"That's okay. I know a sleepy, puffing agent who can fix that parking ticket in short order." Alan laughed and opened the door into the bank President's secretary's office.

"Mr. Baxter is expecting you," the secretary said, pointing to the gold braided door.

Alan opened the door and looked around. "No Nuns or Padres this time?' He asked Baxter.

"I hope not. That Padre wheedled a sizeable contribution from the bank before he left. He kept talking about how it was so great and generous of you to make such a large donation on Police wages. He shamed us into it." Mr. Baxter pushed his chair back from his desk and tossed some bills on the corner next to Alan.

"I don't suppose you can tell us where this came from?' Alan gathered the bills and looked at them. "Yep this is them," he tossed the bills to Bart.

"All I can tell you is that it was in the county money

deposited last night. The county Clerk deposits all the county money. You might get more information from her." Mr. Baxter was ready for the agents to leave.

"You haven't smelled anything like the last setup that bootlegger gave us?" Alan was still Leary.

"No," Mister Baxter looked at his desk and laughed. Alan turned red and bolted toward the door.

"Thank you for your assistance. Call us if you think of anything else." Bart followed Alan. Alan Was brooding and silent all way to the County Clerk's office.

"I can't tell you any specific office the money came through. All the county offices send their deposits here. I give them a receipt and then I deposit the money in the bank. I can tell you what divisions deposited money last night. They will have a copy of the receipts they filled out when they took the money in their offices." The County Clerk leaned on the counter and waited.

Alan shook his head impatiently, more hours

of drudgery. "Is there anyway you can narrow this down?" He asked. "Who deposited the most money yesterday?"

"This is the deadline week for permits so the largest deposits came from the office down the hall that issues the permits. I will give you a list of the county offices depositing in the order of the value of their deposits." The County Clerk was trying to be helpful.

"We'll have to go through them all and decide which ones will help us." Bart smiled ruefully. He knew who was going to be stuck with the lion's share of checking.

After hours of going through and evaluating every cash receipt they received from the county Bart indicated a small pile they had tossed out and check through several times, "I'm inclined to favor the cash from Cleo's used cars. He deposited more than the amount we had out but he deals with the largest cross section of people. He should have recipes for the cash money he took in."

"Yeah I'm thinking the same thing. I'm thinking

that moving as many vehicles as he does would be a good cover for hauling shine also. In view of this I think we should search the premises. Alan rubbed his mouth, "Go to Judge Gaff and see if you can sweet talk him into giving us a search warrant on this meager evidence. Whoever is hauling that moonshine has a good cover or the highway patrol would have caught them by now."

CHAPTER 10

Randy sat in front of the rented apartment window reading a book when the police descended on Cleo's used car lot. He watched Alan and Bart leap from the car and dash into Cleo's office holding their shields in front of them.

Randy reached for the telephone on the coffee table near his chair and dialed the telephone office. "This is the manager of Cleo's used cars I would like to have this number switched from the yard to my home." Randy furnished the need information and hung with a big smile. "Errand boy, huh!" he grunted aloud to himself. Propping his feet up he settled in to enjoy the search going on down the street. Randy could imagine the shock Cleo was having about now.

"What …," Cleo Half rose from his desk.

"Search warrant!" Alan said shoving a paper into Cleo's hand.

"You can't just barge in here and …" Cleo was at loss for words.

"We can, we have and we are." Alan motioned for Cleo to sit down. "You just sit still until we do our work here." Turning to the uniformed officers he said, "Check all the vehicles and shop buildings. You are looking for anything that might be used for transporting moonshine. Pay special attention to all the vehicles as to hidden tanks and verify the contents of all barrels, tanks and containers in the shop buildings. Bart you check Cleo's desk. I'm going to look in the safe for now."

"You can't barge in here and go through my stuff like this." Cleo was getting over the shock of the invasion.

"I'm afraid that piece of paper in your hand said we could. Open the safe for me." Alan ordered.

"Not until my attorney gets here and ok's this invasion as legal." Cleo was desperately trying to think of how he could stall for time.

Bart pushed Cleo and the swivel chair back and began pulling drawers from the desk and riffling through their contents.

"Cut that out!" Cleo demanded.

Bart laughed. "I will, when I'm through."

"Open that safe or I'll call some in who can pick the combination!" Alan lied. "Or better yet, I'll get a welder in here with a cutting torch. A torch will slice through that tin can like a hot knife through butter." Alan was getting a little closer to the truth.

"I don't trust you!" Cleo tried to rise. Bart pushed him back down.

"Bart, bring one of the car salesmen in to witness my search of this safe. Now Cleo open the safe or we cut it open!" Alan ordered.

Cleo stumbled toward the safe. His mind was running a hundred miles an hour. He flubbed the combination a couple of times.

"Come on! Quit stalling. I'm beginning to think

there may be a good reason you don't want me in that safe." Alan was impatient as usual.

Bart looked up and smiled. He loved the way Alan always got into such a tizzy when things didn't go his way. One of these days Alan was going to work himself into a heart attack.

"I have a large amount of money in this safe from a car deal. I don't trust anyone when money is involved, especially the police." Cleo was manufacturing a way out.

The door swung open and Alan pulled Cleo back and dropped to his knees. "Whoo wee," Alan snorted, "Look at all that beautiful money. Bart, clear the top of that desk and get your numbers out." Alan was beside himself. This was it. The big bonanza, "I think we have our bootlegger!"

"I sold an antique automobile for that money. Keep your hands off it," Cleo ordered.

"Not quite," Alan was tossing the bundles of money on the desk. "You sold bootleg booze for this money and I'm about to prove it. Bart, check those top bills."

Bart rolled the bundles of money around and consulted the paper work he had pulled from his pocket. "This is the money from the first plant. I don't see any from the second plant."

Alan glared at Cleo, "Thought you were being smart donating that money to the Widow's and orphan's fund. You knew we'd go charging out there. Well Buddy you're going to pay for that fiasco.

"I don't know what you're talking about I sold a car to a man and he paid in cash." Cleo insisted. 'The man who bought the car wanted to remain anonymous. He said if anybody was to ask his name I should not to give them his name."

"Oh yeah, and I suppose you just happened to lose your copy of the receipt." It was Bart's turn to get sarcastic.

"Oh no, I didn't lose it. It is on top of one of the money bundles. I didn't want to file the receipt until the money was in the bank." Cleo was patting himself on the back for setting this up and hoping he could make it walk.

Bart flipped through the bundles until he found

one that had a receipt on top of it. He read it and silently passed it to Alan.

"Jason Parrott!!" Alan snorted. "Couldn't you have come up with a more original Name?"

"That's the name he gave me. I don't verify the names of cash buyers. There is no law requiring me to verify them." Cleo was seeing a glimmer of hope.

"Come on now!" Alan waved both hands. "We got you. Those boys are going to walk back though those door with the rest of your operation any minute now. Make it easy on yourself and give us the operator's name and the location of that whiskey still. I'll talk to the judge and ask for some clemency for you." Alan was planning on talking to the judge, but go easy was not what he planned to say.

"I know nothing about whiskey or a still," Cleo managed to speak in an aggrieved voice.

The Chief of the outside search party stepped into the doorway. Alan sent a questioning look at him.

The Chief shook his head no and held up both hands, "Nothing" he said.

Alan gulped and sucked in air like he'd been hit in the stomach. His color went from pink to red to white. He'd been so sure when they found the money. Could this be another set up by the Wiley bootlegger? How? Was this bootlegger going make them look like fools again?

Bart smiled at Alan, "Calm down, I don't want to have to drag you out of here. We still have him in custody and possession of the money."

"Finish the search and bring him downtown. We'll interrogate him on our turf." Alan stormed out the door.

"We'll be there in ten minutes." Bart smiled at Alan's back and shook his head. "Old partner," he growled to himself, "You're too nervous for this job." Pointing a finger at Cleo he said, "You better come clean and tell the truth to that man or you'll be eating federal bean for a long time to come. Are you going to walk to that car out there or am I going to have a couple uniformed officers throw you in head first."

"For the thousandth time, I tell you I took that

money in on a car deal. I sold an antique car. I didn't have time to deposit the money in the bank." Cleo rested his head in hands with his elbows on the table. "I need a drink of water. I've been talking to you for hours."

A sharp faced Alan sat across the table, "I sent after you some water. I don't know what the hold up is. Could be they are waiting for the next shift to bring it." Alan chuckled.

"We are checking this car deal out. We'll prove it false so why don't you come clean and give us the information? We'll move you to a comfy cell right now and you can have a drink of water. I'll explain to the judge that you cooperated with us and ask him to go easy with you." Alan drummed his fingers impatiently on the table.

Bart opened the door and motioned Alan from the room. Alan's heart sank. He knew from the look on Bart's face the news wasn't good.

"We found the paper work," Bart pushed an envelope into Alan's hand. "There was a car deal. A Jason Parrott bought a car from Cleo's Used Cars and paid cash. The vehicle number was for a Model T. We haven't been able to locate Jason Parrott or the Model T. We went to the address given and the people never heard of Parrott or the Model T. The boys are canvassing the neighborhood to see if anyone knows anything of Parrott or the Model T.

Bart paused for a breath, "We questioned all Cleo's employees. None knew anything about Parrott. One fellow vaguely remembered an old Junker sitting in the far back corner of the lot but he couldn't even remember if it was a Model T. Anyway, it is gone and it looks like something may have sat there a long time."

The butterflies came alive in Alan's stomach. "Not again," Alan bellowed, "Then it is possible that this slime ball is telling the truth?" he queried.

"I'm afraid the district attorney might think so. I don't believe his story but it's going to take time for us to prove him wrong. We can hold him for a time with the evidence we have. Perhaps we can break his story and get him to confess."

"Move Cleo to a cell and let him cook for awhile.

Keep the boys busy out there. We have to have more evidence. We'll let Cleo cook for awhile then we'll hit him hard," Alan smacked his right fist into his left hand.

Cleo smiled when Bart ordered him escorted to a cell. His plan was working. He patted himself on the back for being smart enough to set it up. It had cost him very little. He'd sold the scrap steel he'd cut the old car into for enough to pay for the gas and oxygen it took to cut the old car up and spent a few dollars paying for the transfer fees on the titles.

Cleo strode confidently down the corridor behind the guard. He was going to beat this case.

"Move over Clyde, you have a new roommate," the guard said as he pushed Cleo into the cell and locked the door.

"What are you in for?" Clyde asked.

"Aw, they're trying to pin a bootlegging thing on me. They can't make it stick. My lawyer is out of town today. I'll be out here by tomorrow night." Cleo was confident his star was rising.

"Were you bootlegging locally?" Clyde asked

softly settling on his bunk. Clyde's slid his hand under the blanket.

It kept niggling and prying at the back of her mind. Vera Lee tossed and turned. Her eyes opened. She looked at the clock. 3:18 AM. Yawning she turned to go back to sleep. A car. There was a car coming up the road. It was crossing the creek.

Slipping a robe over her night gown Vera Lee picked up Jason Marley's revolver and went down stairs to the front door. When the car wheeled up to the gate she was standing in the shadows on the porch.

The door opened and a man exited. Billy Jack! It was Billy Jack. He strode to the gate and hesitated. He opened his mouth to hello the house. He knew the consequences of wandering into a hillbilly house unidentified.

"Billy Jack," Vera Lee said softly and stepped forward to embrace him. Grinning he took the revolver from her hand.

"Vera Lee," Mother questioned softly from the doorway.

"It's Billy Jack mother," Vera Lee answered, "Go back to bed."

"Is something wrong?" Mother questioned.

"Nothing is wrong. I had to bring Vera Lee some business news, Mrs. Marley" Billy Jack's voice was soothing.

"Darn kids have no sense of decency anymore." Mother grumbled to herself as she turned toward her bedroom. "Show up here in the middle of the night, disturbing a body's rest."

"What is wrong?" Vera asked softly so Mother couldn't hear

"The Revenoors have Cleo," Billy Jack informed her. "He was stupid enough to keep the marked money from that first marked money load. They nailed him. I don't know how. And I don't know how much they know."

Vera's knees went weak and she leaned on Billy Jack. "Come to my office. Mother can't hear us there."

"They got Cleo about the time I delivered the last load." Billy Jack settled in a chair in front of

Vera Lee's desk. Opening a window to let the soft night breeze invade the room Vera Lee looked at the chair behind the desk, changed her mind, and drew a chair over near the one Billy Jack sat in. Her knees were weak. She was pale and visibly shaken.

"I watched Randy Simmons pick the load up. He's Cleo's right hand man. He's the one that has always picked the shine up. Randy don't know that I know who he is. I think he's the one who answered the telephone last time I called. I got to thinking about the hello the man said and I didn't think it was Cleo. I'd already stashed the shine so I just watched to see who picked it up.

"As far as I can tell the shine went through the system as usual." Billy jack was silent for a moment. He was very aware of the close proximity of Vera Lee.

"Apparently they didn't arrest Cleo for the whiskey. They arrested him for the money. Damn his sneaky little soul for keeping it!" Vera Lee rose to pace impatiently. "The word I got on the money was that he'd destroyed it. I didn't believe it until you verified the situation. I wonder how the Revenoors learned he had the marked money."

"I don't know how much Cleo knows," Vera Lee was thoughtful. "He was snooping. He was trying to find out who I was. Dad sent one his released prison buddies to discourage him. I do know Cleo is a weasel. He'd sell his Grandmother for a nickel. Either he don't know anything or they haven't made him the best deal he thinks he can get." Vera Lee's pace quickened and her agitation was visibly increasing.

Rising, Billy Jack intercepted Vera Lee at the turning point in her pacing. He pulled her into his arms he kissed her. At first the kiss was tentative, questioning and then grew in intensity.

Vera Lee was shocked and then she melted into Billy Jack's arms. The only person she had ever kissed was David Maloy. This kiss jolted her to a depth she had never known before.

Easing her into a chair Billy Jack dropped to a knee in front of her. "Vera Lee I have loved you since we were children. I spent half my school time daydreaming about you. Let's drop this whiskey business and get married."

"I don't know. You never said anything. I..." Vera Lee was confused.

"You couldn't see anybody but Dave Maloy all our school years." Billy Jack said bitterly. "Your business is thriving. I have watched it diligently for you." Billy Jack rose to pace back and forth. "We can make it grow even more. Close the still and marry me."

"I need more time ... I need a few more loads. Mr. Eisley died and I have to finish the purchase of the Farmer's Market. I ... I." An image of JD Wheeler sitting at the table laughing rose in her mind. This sobered and pulled her back to reality.

Covering her face with both hands she said. "This will have to wait. We have a problem here and we must have a clear head to deal with it. Can you wait for an answer until I have a clear head," Vera Lee implored.

Billy Jack collapsed into a chair, locked his fingers together and stared at the floor. "You can have all the time you need. I have waited a long time. I know what I want."

After a considerable time Billy Jack said, "I don't think they got anything out of Cleo. If they had they would have been swarming on us by now. As far as I know all they have done was lock Cleo up. What Cleo knows and what they can get out of him I don't know."

"The one thing Cleo knows that can be traced back to me is the account number he deposits the money in after each sale. It is not in my name. And I transfer it in cash. The Feds might be able to work out the trail. I hope not." Vera Lee was recovering from the shock of Billy Jack's proposal.

'Cleo hasn't told the Revenoors this yet and he won't tell until it is the last thing he has to deal with. Cleo is a slime ball but he's a clever slime ball. If the money is all they have on him he may weasel out it," Vera Lee reasoned.

"Randy has not deposited the money from the last load yet so he either don't know the number or he is going to try to keep the money." Vera Lee struggled to put the pieces of the puzzle together.

"Do you think we could trust Randy if Cleo goes out of the picture?"

"We can trust Randy about as far as we could trust Cleo. Which is not at all," Billy Jack chuckled.

"Cleo would deposit the money; do you think this Randy will deposit it? We stopped Cleo from snooping do you think Randy can be controlled in this department?" Vera Lee leaned back to look at the light in the ceiling. Her mind was searching for the way out of this predicament.

"If you want, I will run a hundred miles up the road and call the delivery number, and talk to Randy and see what happens. I'll call from a public phone in a large town and if they trace the number it will be ok."

Vera Lee sat with her fingers steepled. Her chin was resting on her thumbs. "That might be the thing to do. I need a few more loads if it can be done. And Randy," Vera Lee rose, "I'll think about the question and I want you to think about it also. To me this is a serious step that must be all or nothing."

"I have thought of nothing else for a long time.

That is the reason I took this job to begin with. That is the reason I have kept track of everyone you deal with. I am sure," Billy Jack turned to the door.

"Billy Jack," Vera Lee said. When Billy Jack stopped and looked back Vera Lee strode over to him and rising onto her toes kissed his cheek. "You be careful and hurry back."

Vera Lee leaned on the porch post and watched the taillights move under the disc of a big round moon and, dipping across the creek, they disappeared into the night. The call of the Great horned Owl passed her ears unheard. The chirp of the cricket and the soft breeze pulling at the bottom of her robe went unnoticed. Her mind was in turmoil and her heart was spinning.

"Is that the young man you have been seeing," Mother's voice came from the doorway.

The sound of mother's voice pulled Vera Lee back to reality once more. "No Mother but you're getting warmer." Vera Lee took mother into her arms and squeezed her hard to stop the questions. "Billy Jack came on an urgent business matter. It has all been settled. How about you making us a good cup of tea," Vera heard the Grandfather clock strike in the recess of the house, "And perhaps a cup of coffee and some of those delightful walnut pancakes. No use going back to bed now. I would never go back to sleep and I need someone to talk to."

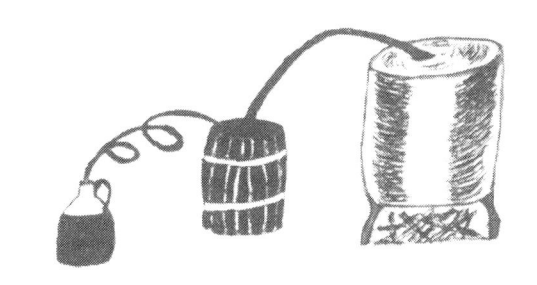

CHAPTER 11

Jason Marley paced the cell from end to end. His parole hearing was coming up.

"I don't think I've seen anybody this wrought up." Jason's cellmate remarked as Jason paced passed him.

"My little girl needs me." Jason muttered.

When Jason came into the prison he was a hard, bitter man. He was as hard on the other prisoners as he was on the guards. The prisoners called him "Crazy Jake". He earned the nick name and spent much of his time in isolation. This suited Jason just fine. His world had been wrecked and turned upside down. He felt he was unjustly punished for making his family a living. He hated the world and he didn't care if the world hated him. He especially hated the guards and anyone else in a uniform with a badge on.

Jason was universally disliked by the prisoners and feared by the guards.

Jason Marley always wanted out but when Vera Lee told him she was going to build a still and bootleg whiskey, getting out became much more important.

Jason paced his cell incessantly. The only way he could see of getting out of this rat hole prison was an early parole. And he sure wasn't going to get it the way things were going.

"The only way out is to convince them I'm a changed man. I have to let them insult me all they want. I have to take it. I have to take it if I want help my little girl." Jason growled to himself. *"I guess I'm going to have to enroll in that anger management class the warden is always pushing. I'll take the class but I ain't going to change.*

"That sorry David Maloy!! None of this would have happened if he had not come back to the valley. I was doing

just fine until he showed up with that tin badge pinned to his shirt. I should have killed him the first day. And to think he was almost my son-in law. If he sends my little girl to prison I will kill him.

"I have to get out so I can claim the still." Jason balled his fist and slammed into the wall, head butting it several times. "I want out," he bellowed loudly.

Jason's cellmate shrank under the blanket. He'd seen other cases of prisoner's getting prison fever and he wanted no part of Jason Marley right now. Jason's roar echoed through the cell block and the other prisoners knew what Jason was going through.

The guards were sitting around a card table when Jason's cry bounced from wall to wall past them. The guard holding aces and eights smiled, "That's Jason Marley. You boys be careful when we march them to the breakfast table."

Jason was acutely aware of the two burly guards standing behind him while he ate breakfast. The guards marched back to the cell block with him.

"Marley Stand in the hall," the guard with the close cropped blond hair and the thin little Hitler mustache ordered. All the other prisoners entered their cell and the doors on each cell closed.

"Marley it has come to my attention that the floor in the hall of this cell block is filthy. You see the bucket in the corner yonder," the blond guard pointed a blunt finger. "You take that bucket and the brush in it and you scrub this floor! I want it spotless!"

The other guard moved to the opposite side of Jason, prepared for the explosion. Jason seemed to swell and grow taller. His fists balled. He looked at the ceiling and then the floor. He exhaled and deflated. His shoulders sank. Looking at the Hitler mustache he mumbled, "Yes sir," and shuffled toward the bucket.

The guards gave each other a startled disappointed look. They like to prove how tough they were by manhandling a prisoner. What was this? One of their toughest prisoners saying, "Yes Sir?"

Jason dropped to his knees and began to scrub the floor. The guards exchanged an "I don't believe this look" and walked away frowning in disappointment.

A prisoner leaned on the bars of his cell and watched the guards pass through the locking doors at the end of the cell block. "Jake, I don't believe this, if it were me, I'd have taken my beating and spent six months in solitary before I'd have scrubbed that floor. I thought you would have done the same."

Jason turned even redder. He lowered his head and scrubbed harder and faster. He was fighting for control with all his might. Sweat dripped off his brow into the water. His face was blood red and the fingers held the brush in so fierce a grip they turned white. The brush was making a loud swishing sound as Jason swung it around. He must, just must stay out of trouble. It had to start somewhere and this was it. "Hang on!" he ordered himself.

One of the prisoners stuck his arms through the bars and rested them on the cross bars. He began to sing in a high mocking voice, "Mary had a dirty little floor. Where ever the guard pointed Jason was sure to go."

"Mary had a little lamb," Jason rose to his feet, "Where Mary went the lamb was sure to go," Jason was waltzing along waving his arms like he was leading an orchestra. When he passed the singing prisoner's cell he slid his left hand through the bars. Seizing the prisoner's hair he jerked the prisoner's face violently into the bars. There was an audible crunch.

The prisoner started to sink. Jason's right hand caught the prisoner's right hand in a tight hand shake position. Rising to his toes Jason dropped his full weight on the arm resting on the cross bar. The loud crack of the breaking bones echoed down the cell block. The prisoner screamed in mortal pain.

Jason released flopping arm and dropped to his scrub brush. The door flew open and the blond with the Hitler mustache was leading the charge. He came to an abrupt stop. Jason was scrubbing the floor and all the other prisoners were going about their business.

"What is going on here?" he demanded stepping up close to Jason. There were no answers. There was no sign any of the prisoners heard the question.

"What is wrong with you?" The guard demanded

of the prisoner who lay moaning on his bunk. He was holding his right arm in his left hand. The right arm had a ninety degree bend in the forearm.

"My arm is broken," the prisoner moaned.

"Yeah, and your face is split open like you butted the bars. I suppose you're going to tell me you slipped on the soap and fell into the bars." The guard was staring at Jason. What do you know about this Marley?" The Guard asked.

"I heard a loud scream and saw him crawling upon the bunk." Jason continued to scrub.

"I did slip and fall into bars." The injured prisoner groaned.

"Yeah, yeah." The guard turned to the silent guards standing behind him. "Take this wounded yeahu down to Doc Simmons. "Search his cell and while you're at it search Marley's cell also."

Marley kept his head down and scrubbed the floor vigorously. The guards led the wounded prisoner out of the cell block. When the cell block doors slammed shut Jason sat back on his heels and looked up and down the cell block. A new respect for him had been born in both prisoners and guards.

"Sorry Jake," the first prisoner said, "I know you have a reason for not splitting the little Hitler wide open."

Bart sat dozing at his desk when Alan bustled in. "Come on, wake up. Gee don't you ever go to bed and sleep? Let's go get Cleo. Why don't you already have him up here? I'm sure that weasel has had time to think up a deal. We're going to find out where that Bootlegger's still is today." Alan was almost cheerful this morning.

Clattering down the stairs two at a time Alan was followed by the puffing Bart.

Alan held his badge at arms length toward the guard at the table, "let us in and open the door to cell 6," he ordered.

"You aren't going to like it." The guard never moved.

"What?" Alan bumped the door he expected to fly open at his approach.

"Your boy in cell six is dead." The guard said matter of factly.

'What! He can't be. We sent him down yesterday. He was OK then, what did he do? Hang himself?" Alan sputtered. Staggering to a chair he plopped down. It hit him like a ton of bricks. He placed his face in his hands. They were back to square one again. Was there no justice? He thought.

Bart lost his sleepy look. "What happened to Cleo?" Bart was looking the guard in the eye with a no nonsense allowed stance. A hand rested on his hip.

The guard couldn't standup to Bart's gaze he dropped his eyes. He didn't like these agents anyway. He tried for the Academy and was turned down.

The Highway Patrol turned him down also. He knew he deserved better than prison guard.

"Well nobody knows yet." The guard pushed his chair back. "The morning bed check found him lying on the floor next to the bars. His throat had been cut. They found a prisoner made shiv in the middle of the hall. Whither he cut his own throat or somebody cut it for him remains to seen. A coroner and a prison team are on their way down to investigate it. Anyway, I can let you in but don't touch or move anything."

"Thanks for the lesson in police work," Alan said sarcastically." He motioned Bart toward the door.

The guard pushed buttons and the doors opened.

The body lay as advertized. The amount of blood across and up and down the hall indicated Cleo held onto the bars or was held against the bars while bleeding out.

Alan glanced at the bunk Cleo's cellmate was laying on. "CLYDE," he bellowed. "What are you doing in this cell?"

"This is the one they put me in. I had no choice. This ain't the Hilton you know." Clyde was sullen.

"What did you do to Cleo?" Alan demanded.

"I didn't do anything to Cleo." Clyde was defensive. "I went to sleep and when I woke up he was there on the floor."

Alan's back straightened and his hands quivered.

Bart took Alan by the arm and turned him toward the door. "No one knew or now knows you told Clyde the Bootlegger killed Rudy. They may not find out.

They had no reason not to put Cleo in that cell. We need to get out of here. We got Clyde now. He will tell us everything."

Alan reluctantly followed Bart out of the cell block.

Billy Jack listened to the whirr of the telephone ringing on the pay phone hand set.

"Hello," Randy was expecting this call.

"Randy, you took the last load of shine. You still have our money." Billy Jack kept the tone flat and even.

"How did you know my name? Did Cleo tell you?" Randy was worried.

"We know all about you. Who you are and what you do. We know and can adjust any part of this operation." Billy Jack kept his voice even and dead flat.

"If you know all this, you know I was Cleo partner and I can handle operations on this end. Cleo got greedy and careless. He kept the marked money thinking he'd turn a profit on it somehow.

"The Feds only got the money. They got nothing

on the operation. If I know Cleo he was too much of a weasel to tell them anything he knew on the first day. If he had any information he'd try to make a deal. Cleo ain't going to make a deal with anybody he is dead." Randy waited to see how this news affected the voice on the line.

"Cleo died?" this was news to Billy Jack.

"Yeah, they put him in the cell with a customer of mine's friend and the fellow cut Cleo's throat." Randy waited. He really wanted to do business with this voice on the phone. But he knew better than to push it.

After a long silence the voice came back. "Do you have a pencil?"

"Yes," Randy smiled. They were going to do business with him.

"You deposit our money in account number 1783489747 at the First National Bank. We will weigh the situation and I will get back with you." Billy Jack hung the hand set up before Randy had time to answer. He had spent too much time at the pay phone it was time to move.

Billy Jack didn't like the situation at all. He didn't like doing business with Randy at all. He had never met the man face to face but he could feel the sneaky in him.

If the Revenoors were to catch him, Billy Jack knew that as a second offender he was going up for a long spell. There was a lot places he had rather be. The businesses Vera Lee established to cover the whiskey making and transporting moonshine were growing rapidly and doing well. They could make it without the moonshine. One thing for sure, he was not leaving without Vera Lee. He was head over heels in love with her. He'd always been fond of her, even when she only had eyes for David Maloy. That fondness had blossomed and grown while working with and advising her on the moonshine operation.

Vera Lee said she needed a few more loads. Perhaps he could talk her into ending it soon. He was feeling the heat from the Revenoors. His instincts were saying Bail out now.

Half block up the street he wheeled into a drive in food place. He parked where he had a full view of the pay phone he'd just left. If his Call had been traced there should be someone showing in up in the area very soon.

"Cheese Burger, Fries and a coke." He told the pretty little carhop when she wheeled up to his car on her roller skates.

Billy Jack took his time devouring the Cheese Burger. He watched the cars on the street. He studied each parked car looking for an unseen occupant. He especially scrutinized a lady who used the phone after he left. She was a fashion plate leading a highly manicured poodle dog. Billy Jack decided there was no harm in her. He wondered how much money was in the Loomis Armored Car parked in front of the Bank a block down the street.

By the time Billy Jack finished the hamburger he had found nothing that look remotely suspicious. He turned his headlights on and when the carhop removed the tray from his window he tipped her generously.

He decided to go see Vera Lee and return to Nebraska immediately. He wanted to keep an eye on Randy as much as possible.

Alan leaned back and rubbed his hands down his face. "What else can go wrong with this case?" He sighed.

"Well," Bart said, "We know the moonshine is being manufactured somewhere else and is being transported into our district for sale. We have checked this district to death. We've have checked the ingredient stores and companies. We've hit all our stool pigeons. The people we've caught bootlegging know nothing. They're buying blind and the traps we have set backfired on us." Bart paused. "We're dealing with a smart cookie."

"You would think we could have found out something on the transport of the moonshine by now." Alan mused.

"We know this moonshine is being made in another district. We need to ask the Federal director to bring all the district directors in and put them to checking their districts."

"Not yet," Alan was quick to answer. "We have Clyde. He is in big trouble and he knows it. Perhaps he will come through with something.

"I want go over this Cleo characters: bank records, business records and his personal records. I'm going to get to know him better than I know my brother. I want his place of business gone over by experts. He has to be tied in with this moonshine ring. Don't call for help yet we'll get this crafty weasel yet."

CHAPTER 12

Vera Lee drew doodles, loops and circles on a legal pad. She was tired and it showed. She had not been sleeping well since Cleo's arrest. The realization of how fragile her life was had come home to roast. Henry Eisley sat halfway down the table, resting his chin on laced fingers, watching the parking lot. Ruby Rail sat, engrossed in paperwork, across the table from Vera Lee. J.D. Wheeler and Robin sat at the opposite end of the table in animated conversation.

Mister Eisley had willed the Farmer's Market to both Henry and Alma before passing on. J.D set this meeting to sign the final papers on the sale of the

Farmer's Market.

Walter and Alma were late as usual. Henry looked at his watch and shook his head when they slipped into a parking space in front of J.D's. office.

When the hustle and bustle of getting everyone seated behind the right bundle of paperwork on the desk was over J.D. began, "Ruby Rail, A real estate broker, is here to represent Robin and Versa Lee in the purchase of this property. I have prepared the paperwork for Vera Lee and Robin's partnership and co-ownership of the store. We will have them sign these contracts and agreements. This will make them a legal entity and then we'll proceed with the paperwork for the sale of the store to this partnership."

"There is one other thing we should discuss before we sign." Walter rose to a standing position. "The value of the store has increased dramatically since we last met. There has to be an adjustment in the sale price before Alma signs these papers."

"You signed a contract that you would sell at this price if you inherited the store." J.D. reminded

Walter.

"Yeah, but then we were hoping to get the entire store. We only got half of it. We need more money. There must be an increase in the sale price." Walter asserted puffing up his chest like a carrier pigeon.

"Bull!" All Vera Lee's fear and resentment of the past few days came boiling to the surface. Leaping to her feet she placed both hands on the table and leaned toward Walter. With her lips drawn thin her dark eyes bore into Walter. Her voice was a seething whisper. "You try this and we'll sue you. I'll have J.D. tie the store up, closed, for about three years and we'll ask for a large chunk of money for lost business, damage to the business, punitive damage and lawyer fees. Then when we've been granted all this, and you can bet your bottom dollar we will be, we will bail out on you and leave you with a store that will be a worthless piece of junk.

"Now you hold ..." Walter began

"No! You hold on," Vera Lee's hissed. Pointing a demanding finger to Walter's chair she said, "Sit down in that chair and sign those papers or hit that door running and face the legal action sure to follow. This is not a negotiable item." Her eyes and body language said no compromise.

Walter looked at Alma and J.D. he was seeking help anywhere he could get it.

"Walter," Henry rose from the table also. "If you blow this deal I'm going to sue you too. If you blow this deal and get us involved in a drawn out lawsuit I'll lose money, you will be hip deep in lawyer fees, and when the dust settles you will owe these folks a bundle and the store will be worthless. Sit down and sign those papers!"

Walter looked at Alma again. She was panic stricken. The thought of coming out of this with no money after the big plans she'd built hit her like a runaway freight train. Overcome she leaned forward and covered her face with her hands.

"There are other people interested. We can get more money for the business." Walter was still defiant. He had spent hours planning this attack. He'd gone so far as to have his friends make up fake written offers for the store that were much higher than the price he'd sign to sell it at. He reached for these offers.

"Walter," J.D. leaned back in his chair. He held each ends of a pencil in his hands and rolled it up and down between his fingers and thumbs. He spoke in a quiet assured official manner, "Miss Marley is right Walter, you signed a binding contract. If you try to renege on that contract; I will sue and, if Miss Marley requests, I can close the store and delay the case in court for perhaps four years.

"By that time all the stock in the store will be worse than worthless. It will have to be destroyed. Loss of stock, the cost of removing and destroying the same will be highly expensive. In the meantime I will see you pay the taxes. You will pay to maintain the building and grounds.

"We will sue for moneys the store would have made while it's closed. We will sue for lose of stock and the cost of disposing said stock plus cleanup. We will sue for loss of business good will. By the time this gets to court I will have thought of a few more items to add to this list.

"In this state the courts can find that a person has negligently and capriciously harmed another. If the court finds this has happened it can award a total of four times the damage. Due to this law I'd say in about four years you will give Miss Marley and Robin the building and grounds along with enough money to restock it. Perhaps some of the other property holdings you have around town will be affected. I will be looking into your net worth," J.D. rolled the pencil and waited.

Alma was openly in tears. Walter stood with his mouth working and his finger waving but no words were coming out. This was not the way he'd imagined it would work. He thought he could show the offers he now had in his hand and bully more money out of these women. He thought he might get Vera Lee to match the offer and if this didn't work he would graciously offer to settle by splitting the difference. He looked wildly around the room for help or an idea. None came.

"Sit down and sign!" Henry demanded.

Slowly and silently Walter sank into the chair and

picking up the pen handed it to Alma.

The actual signing only took minutes. J.D. and Robin were in a celebratory mood. They were laughing and high fiving.

"Boy, remind me to never get Vera Lee mad at me. Did you see the way she ate the bully out of old Walter? I thought he was going to have a heart attack there for a minute." Robin laughed.

"Yeah, I held my breath there for a moment. I was afraid he'd call Vera Lee's bluff and walk out. Instead he just melted and signed." J.D. looked at his watch, "I took the liberty of reserving a celebration dinner table at the best restaurant town. We will be a little late but I think it will OK."

"I wasn't bluffing. I was telling." Vera Lee still sat at the table. The fires of anger had burned out and left the taste of ashes in her mouth. She felt so low she would have to look up to see a snake's belly, "I think I will take a rain Check. I have something I need to do."

"Are you ok?" A suddenly worried Robin leaned on the table.

"I'm ok." Vera Lee cast a quick glance at J.D. "You two go and have fun." Then she winked at Robin.

When the door closed behind the disgustingly happy Robin and J.D. Vera Lee lay her head on the table. *Billy Jack, where are you when I need you?* She thought.

Two burly guards escorted Clyde from the cells to the table in the interrogation room. Clyde walked crab like and stooped from the weight and constriction of the chains and restraints.

Alan and Bart sat behind the table. A fresh cup of coffee sat in front of them and another cup sat across the table from them. "Take those off," Alan motioned to the restraints Clyde was wearing, "And you boys wait outside. We'll holler when we need you."

Everyone sat and silently listened to the clatter and clash of the chains and restraints being removed. The officers gathered the rattling restraints and left the room.

"Have a seat." Alan motioned toward the seat with the coffee sitting in front of it and forced himself to be civil.

Clyde sat, smelled and sipped the coffee. Holding the cup up he smiled, "You boys drink a lot better coffee than they serve in the cell block."

"Don't they feed you right?" Bart looked like he was half asleep.

"They feed us slop but I'm sure you didn't bring me up here to have coffee break and discuss cell block food with you." Clyde sipped the coffee again. "This is good coffee."

"We brought you in here to try to save your posterior. You are charged with murder one. In this state that carries the death penalty. You help us and we can help you with the D.A. We'll help each other."

"I already helped you. I killed that dirty bootlegger that killed my buddy Rudy," Clyde sipped the coffee. "I saved the state a lot of money for his trial."

"Unless you make a deal and tell us who made that whiskey and where he makes it your trial will cost the state a lot more. They do it with a needle in the arm now days." Alan's inpatients was showing.

"Not to mention those long days in a cell on death row."

"I already told you. Rudy called me and asked for help picking up a load of booze. I went with him and helped. Those deputies got us before we got home. That is all I know. If I knew more I'd be dealing with you. I can't tell you something I don't know."

Alan looked at Bart. Bart sat with an elbow on the table with his face lying on his hand. He was bored with the situation. Alan turned back to Clyde, "If you stick to this story there is nothing we can do for you." Alan turned to the door "Guards," He yelled.

"Well," Alan said when the guards finished trussing Clyde and left the room with him. "We're not going to get anything out of him. Either he don't know anything or he will not tell."

"I think he's telling the truth." Bart still leaned with his elbow on the table. "Who could he be protecting? If he knew anything worthwhile he'd be trying to get the best deal out of us and the DA."

"Now we go through Cleo's office. There has to a crack in this case somewhere. We will find it if we keep looking."

"Whoopee! That sounds like fun." Bart still rested his face in his hand and waved one finger at the ceiling and swung it around in a circular motion. "I'll take his financial transactions and you check his car sales." *I'm not going to do it all this time, Bart thought.*

"I was planning on looking at his friends and acquaintances." Alan said.

"We'll have a better idea who these friends and acquaintances are after we go through his business and financial records." Bart countered. "Those last two bootleggers we caught peddling "shine" bothered me, especially the fat lady on edge of town. They had a different feel."

I had a chemical analyst test ran on the whiskey we took from her. He said it was made at a different location than the first we tested. There was more sulfur and gypsum in the water it was made with."

"Oh Great!" Alan held up his hands. "Are you thinking of a traveling still that makes a batch and moves to a different location or are you thinking another still has began operating in our area?"

Bart considered the question, "Feels like another still." He said. "Let's go get Cleo's office and get that over with. That is one thing I don't like about this job."

Alan tried to think of a way to get Bart to do the drudge work, he surrendered. He'd worked with this partner too long. Bart had his mind made up. This was the way it was going to be.

"We're in the wrong business." Alan tossed the folder on top of the large pile of folders on the desk. "This guy sold a lot of cars. Of course he was so crooked I bet he had to screw his pants on every morning."

"Are you done? I finished the financial investigation this morning and compiled a list of Cleo's employees." Bart sat a stack of paperwork down and plopped into a chair.

"I found a little stuff the State boys might be interested in but I found nothing to tie him to the bootlegger." Alan was feeling low.

"The old boy made a good bit of money on the

cars he sold. I couldn't find where he had any money or way of life that indicated he was making money elsewhere. Of course we know this fellow was a sharp weasel. He may have a safe or loose board in floor where he stashes cash money planning to retire to the Bahamas someday." Bart mused.

Alan's head snapped up. "You may have something there," He said reaching for the phone. "I'll get a warrant for the forensic team to take this place apart looking for a hidden safe, a loose floorboard, a hole in the sheetrock or any other place large amounts of currency could be stored. We better put Cleo's house on the search list also. You better check all the banks in town to see if he had a safety deposit box. Can you think of any other place Cleo might have stashed money?"

"You better sit down and give this some thought," Bart smiled at Alan's agitation. "Remember this guy has made us look like fools a couple of times."

Alan cast a dirty look at Bart and growled.

"I'll set up an interview with all Cleo's employees and friends." Bart cranked a sheet into Cleo's secretary's typewriter.

Jason Marley pushed through the door. His two guards took up station on either side of the door. "This is a waste of time and effort one growled to the other."

There was a chair sitting beside the door. Jason sat in it. He was going to take this anger management class but he wasn't going to like it. It was just another step to getting out of prison to help his little girl. She was playing with fire and Jason didn't want her hurt or worse yet be thrown into a place like this.

The correctional officer teaching the class looked up and smiled. He had placed the chair near the door just for Jason. The warden warned him about Jason.

The teacher rose and walking around his desk with both hands flat against each other in front of him said, "Welcome to the class. We have a new comer today. Jason Marley, welcome to the class." The teacher watched Jason's face turn red.

Dropping his hands the teacher continued, "About six centuries ago Buddha said, "If you know your enemy and yourself, you can win every battle without jeopardy."

Get hold of yourself, sit still and keep your mouth shut, Jason scolded, *you are going to go through the motions and pass this class if you want out of here.* Jason locked his jaws and pulled his stubborn will to the breaking point. He sat dead still.

That night Jason lay in his bunk with Buddha's words bouncing through his mind. How can a man's words, uttered six or eight centuries ago, echo off the walls of history down to the present date? It must be the simple truth of the words. Or was it human nature's wistful way of thinking?

Who was this Buddha fellow anyway? Jason had never heard of him. *I'll have to ask the instructor who this Buddha fellow is,* Jason thought and dozed off to sleep thinking of something beside how to even the score between him, David Maloy and the Judge who sentenced him to this God forsaken place.

Jason built a mental guard against the Hitler mustache and his henchmen. Every time he saw the mustache he conjured up an image of Vera Lee in her pink princess costume for the fourth grade play, prancing across the stage with her dainty little nose in the air.

While they were deriding, humiliating and insulting him he smiled and, in his minds eye, counted Vera Lee's steps across the stage.

Lead by the Hitler mustache, the sadistic guards razzed and harassed him for a time and then moved on to new more volatile prisoners for their pleasure.

The prisoner's word on the cell block was; don't mess with Jason Marley. He will get you when you least expect it.

As time went by Jason did change. His iron will, the anger management class and its teacher bent the direction of his life.

When he first entered prison a fight with a prisoner or guard just gave vent to his frustration. He knew he was going to lose all those fights but giving a smart mouthed guard a bloody nose or black eye was considered a victory. The beatings he took were of no consequence to him. Being a solitary man, getting thrown into isolation raised no special terror in his breast. At times he welcomed it.

He was a bitter dangerous man at this stage of his life. It was possible for him to kill in a fit of anger. The guards and prisoners recognized this and were afraid.

Using his warrior blood and iron will he turned all this in on himself. He made himself be humble and take the jabs and insults of the Hitler moustache group.

As time went by he began to see the advantages of holding his temper and developed methods and means to corral his temper to an extent. He was looking forward to the next Parole Board meeting.

Jason sat on the edge of the chair nervously trying to peer into the Parole Board hearing room to get a glance at the people who were going to decide his fate each time a prisoner went in or came out.

CHAPTER 13

For sometime after Robin and J.D. departed Vera Lee sat with her head on the table. Raising her head Vera Lee took up the pencil. Her doodles now became facts and figures.

We own the store now, she thought, two columns of figures appeared. *The bakery has been free and clear for a long time but the remodeling of the store to accommodate the bakery is expensive.* Two more columns of figures appeared. *The logging company has done well since Carl became involved,* two more columns. *The furniture factories, Billy Jack has done an unbelievable ...,* she stopped.

Holding the pencil by both ends she chewed

on the middle. A vision of Billy Jack as a school boy chasing her across the school grounds with a garter snake in his hand passed before her eyes. And then there was the big hated cowboy booted teenage Billy Jack, driving hot cars, hauling bootleg whiskey and thumbing his nose at the Revenoors. A pang of jealousy shot through her as remembered all the girls swooning over his show off flamboyant character. The grave, level headed Billy Jack of today floated before her eyes. Seated behind his desk, dressed in his immaculate business suit, he still had all the women swooning over him. A bigger pang of jealousy shot through her.

Vera Lee jerked herself back to reality. *Billy Jack has done fabulously well in our lumber sales and furniture manufacture business.* She added two more columns of figures.

Adding and subtracting Vera Lee juggled the figures this way and that. The figures painted a rosy picture. *The profits off ten more loads of shine, with what I have and Robin is putting in, will clear the store.*

"I'm going to shut the still down," Vera Lee

decided aloud, "I'm going to marry Billy Jack and then move to Nebraska."

Move to Nebraska? The thought startled her. One of the main problems between her and Dave Maloy had been her stubborn refusal to leave the valley.

Now, are you willing to toss it and go? She asked herself. For the first time she was willing admit her love for Dave Maloy had been a teenage infatuation without the deep meaning of true love. This shocked her to her shoe toes. She'd spent years hating Lesa for stealing Dave from her. Suddenly she realized Dave had been smart enough to recognize the extent and depth of their relationship and end it. The feelings ran so deep she shook as if chilled.

Versa Lee committed herself to saying yes to Billy Jack's proposal and going where he went. With this decision made she picked up her bundle of the paperwork and headed for home. There was much stuff she needed to discuss with mother.

Dinner was ready when Vera Lee arrived home. The sight of the table stopped Vera Lee in her tracks.

A frilly, lacey, embroidered tablecloth draped the table. Two Chrystal candle holders on either end of the table supported the candles standing guard over the ancient fine china set carefully around the table. Highly polished real silver silverware rested beside each plate.

It was a sight Vera Lee had only seen a couple of times in her entire life. Jason purchased the china and silverware from a traveling salesman, many, many years ago as a present for Ruth. Ruth guarded it with her life ever since. It only came out of its hiding place on super special occasions.

The scent of roast beef, Vera Lee's favorite meal, floated to her nose. *Aha*, she thought, *I told mother we were closing the deal for the store today so she is making a celebration of the event.*

Vera Lee managed to hold her news in check while they enjoyed the meal. Dabbing at her mouth with the napkin she placed it on the table, pushing her plate away. It had been a filling and enjoyable meal.

"Mother, I have some news," Vera began

tentatively and hesitated.

"Billy Jack proposed?" Mother smiled.

"Did he tell you?" Vera Lee's face flamed red.

"No, he did not tell me! Don't go getting your skirts in a snit!" Mother declared.

"How did you know he proposed?" Vera Lee was curious.

"Are you forgetting I'm the woman who used to change your diapers?" Mother asked.

Vera Lee laughed. "No mother, I have not forgotten. You always have read me like an open book. Billy Jack did propose."

"Well …?" Mother cocked her head and waited.

"I told him I'd consider it and give him an answer." Vera Lee said.

"And …?" Mother watched her intently.

"I've considered it and I'm going to marry him." Vera Lee gushed.

"Oh," Mother gasped. Leaping from her chair she ran around the table and hugged Vera Lee intensely.

"When is the wedding going to be?" Pulling a

chair in front Vera Lee mother sat down.

"Mother! I haven't even accepted his proposal yet," Vera Lee protested. "I'll get married and we'll move to Nebraska. We'll build a new home there. We will have electricity and all the conveniences. There will be stores so close we can walk to them." Vera Lee was planning as she went.

Mother's face took on a startled look which faded into a deeply concerned expression. She rose and clatteringly gathering the fine china moved to the sink. Placing the dishes in the sink she turned. Her face was gray.

"Do you mean leave my home?" Mother asked softly.

"Yes, we'll build a wonderful house in Penwick. It will be nice there." Vera Lee was growing concerned. It never occurred to her that mother would not want to go with her.

Mother staggered back, groped for the chair and then plopped into it. "This is my home," she rocked to and fro. "This is the house Jason brought me to when we married. This is the house you were born in. Those little hand prints on the door facing are yours. I never let that door facing be painted."

"You can design the kitchen just the way you want it. We'll have so much fun designing the new house and buying new furniture." Vera Lee tried again.

"No," mothers jaw set, "I'm not leaving my home."

Vera Lee didn't know what to say. It had been so clear when she walked through the door a little while back. Leaning forward she put her arms around her mother. "We'll work it out some how." She said lamely.

"Thank you for coming in. We appreciate your co-operation." Alan dismissed Cleo's top salesman.

"That is the last of the employees and so far this has been a bust. We haven't picked up anything new. Is it possible Cleo was telling the truth? Did he sell a car for that money?" Bart's arm rested on Cleo's desk and he gazed through the open door. A policeman writing a speeder a ticket had stopped to gaze at a young lady leading a dog on the sidewalk.

"You know better than that. The name he gave us doesn't exist. We'll find the connection yet. Who is the first of Cleo's friends? We'll get something there." Alan wasn't about to give up.

"A list of Cleo's friends is easy to go through. He cheated everyone he came into contact with. A list of his friends is easy to get through. We have an appointment, a Randy Simmons, in thirty minutes. I don't know about you but I'm going to take a nap," Bart yawned.

Randy dressed with care. Studying his profile in the mirror he took his shirt off and wadded it into a ball and put it back on. It had just the proper wrinkles he was looking for. He was going to need his 'forgotten man look' more today than ever. He must convince these Revenue Agents he knew nothing of Cleo's business dealings. It should be easy to convince them he knew nothing of Cleo's legal business because he did not know anything about it. Cleo always dealt from close to the vest.

Randy had known Cleo since kindergarten. Even then, Cleo had been a bully figuring how to take his classmates' lunch money. Randy hung at Cleo's elbow and took the easy pickings Cleo missed or created

Cleo was happy to keep Randy at his elbow. Occasionally he would purposely leave a deal hanging Randy could profit from. It was down right handy to have a man you could trust.

Alan slammed the phone down, "No luck," and shook his head. "They searched Cleo's house and found nothing. The warrant covered the entire property. They even probed the flower pots and came up with nothing to even tie him to the car yard. The guy took none of his work home with him. He must not have trusted his wife."

Bart shuffled through his notes from the previous interviews with Cleo's employees. He came up with nothing of note. He was refreshed from the nap. Alan had gotten a little loud on the phone or he'd still be napping. Bart looked up to see a man peeking around the facing of the open door.

"Come in," Bart laid the folders on Cleo's desk and motioned with his hand.

Randy snatched the hat from his head and slid around the door facing like a mouse looking for a cat. Clutching the hat to his chest Randy treaded softly across the floor he stopped in front of Cleo's desk. "I'm Randy Simmons," he announced.

"Have a seat," Bart motioned to an empty chair beside the desk, "We asked you here because we have some unanswered questions about Cleo and his business dealings. I understand you and Cleo were friends?"

"I went to school with Cleo and have known him for many years. Cleo was a hard man to be friends with. He didn't have many friends. He wasn't very honest and he trusted no one." Randy's eyes fell to his shoe toes and he continued to clutch the hat.

"What kind of relationship did you have with Cleo?" Bart leaned back in his chair.

"Well," Randy laid the hat in his lap and hesitated, "Cleo and I went to school together. When we graduated I went to work for the county and Cleo went into the used car business. He did well at it.

"Over the years I've bought several vehicles from him. He always gave me a good deal. I guess it was because we went to school together and over the years I've sent several customers to him. He always paid me a commission when I sold a car for him."

Alan took a seat at the other end of the desk. Randy avoided eye contact with both Bart and Alan

"You worked for Cleo then?" Bart continued.

Randy looked at the ceiling, scratched his head, held both hands up, and said, "I suppose so. You might say I worked part time over the years. If his janitor didn't show up he'd call me and I'd come down and do the job at night. I did odd jobs occasionally. If I sold a car he paid me a commission."

"You did oddball stuff then?" Bart waved his pencil in a circle. "How often did you go to Cleo's house for picnics, dinners or what have you?"

"Are you kidding? Randy's head jerked up and he looked Bart in the eye. "You didn't know Cleo. He was too much of a skinflint to have anyone over for a Bar-B-Que. Beside that, his wife would have killed him if he'd pulled the unwashed into her social circle."

"Do you know a Jason Parrott?" Alan was getting impatient.

"Jason Parrott?" Randy searched his mind.

"Yeah, He bought an Antique Model T from Cleo." Alan interjected

So this is how Cleo tried to cover having the marked money in his safe! Randy's quick wit latched onto this fact like the slamming of a bear trap. He looked at his toes and put all his will power into looking like he was searching through a slow mind for Jason Parrott.

This was dangerous ground. He was supposed to know nothing of the money but this had possibilities. Perhaps he could send these feds off on a false trail. He remembered an old Model T that used to sit in the back of the lot. "I don't remember any Jason Parrott But I do remember an old model T."

"Do you remember what happened to it?" Alan was fully alert.

"Sure do, Cleo paid me fifty bucks to deliver it to Plunketville." Randy said.

Even Bart was alert. "Who did you deliver it to?"

"Some funky kid in a leather jacket," careful now, Randy cautioned himself don't remember too much.

"What was the address you delivered to?" Alan asked.

"No address. You know there is only one store in Plunketville. He met me in front of the store." Randy picked the hat up and stared at it blankly as if trying to remember.

"How did you get home?"

"I drove Cleo's truck home. I hauled the old car over on Cleo's car hauler." Randy answered.

"When was this?" Alan asked.

Randy tired to remember the date the dog took the marked money. He put on a convincing show. He was asking himself what day Cleo would have set this subterfuge up on? Bart and Alan thought he was trying to remember the delivery date. "I can't remember the exact date but it some time ago."

"Give me description of this punk kid in the leather jacket," Bart picked up a pen.

"I don't know he was just a punk kid. He had a leather jacket and levis." Randy looked around batting his eyes and pretending to look inside for the memory, "He was eighteen or nineteen, he had one of those ducktail hair cuts and a smart mouth."

"How tall was this kid and what color was his hair?" Bart asked.

"He was a couple inches taller than me and had dark hair," Randy was storing all this in his memory in case he was asked again.

"Which way did he go when he left?" Alan asked.

"I don't know he was leaning against the old car drinking a beer when I left." Randy was going over this description again in his mind.

"Do you know where Cleo kept his money?" Alan asked

Randy was thoughtful for a moment, "He always paid me with a check when I did something for him. I guess he kept his money in the bank. Cleo was a close man. He never told anyone much."

"Do you know if he kept money in more than one bank?" Alan persisted adamantly.

Randy cringed, avoided eye contact and looked at his shoe toe. "Like I told you, Cleo had no friends. To Cleo there were only two types of people. Those he could cheat out of a dollar and those he could use to cheat the first with."

"Were all the checks he wrote you on the same bank?" Alan's voice dripped with the frustration he was feeling. He could see the dead end coming again.

Shrugging his shoulders Randy continued to look at the floor. "A check is a check. I only looked at the dollar amount. I didn't look to see which bank it was written on."

Alan rose placed a hand on each hip, strode to a window and stared down the street. Bart closed the folder on the desk and smiled at Alan's back. They had been partners for several years. He was truly fond of Alan but Alan's frustration never failed to fully amused the easy going Bart. "Mister Simmons, thank you for coming in. We may be contacting you later."

"Milksop," Alan turned from the window to watch Randy's receding back.

"Off to Plunketville." Bart tossed the folders into a briefcase and slammed the lid.

Alan eased the government Ford off the highway onto the dirt lot in front of a dilapidated old wood store building that had lived much longer than it should have. A faded barely readable sign hanging above the "Drink Coca-cola" sign declared the place to be Plunketville. The Post Office had been removed years before. Only its distance from any other business kept the old store alive. The local farmers and ranchers buying minor stuff they ran out, or the gallon of milk they forgot while they were in town kept the old building alive.

The screen door screeched and the wood floor thumped hollowly under their tread. The old man dozing in a chair leaning against the wall behind the counter was about as old and dilapidated as the store.

"Come in here," the old man greeted them bringing the chair back to four legs with a thump. "What can I do for you?"

Bart flashed his badge and identification. "We'd like to ask you if you saw a punk kid in here with a ducktail haircut."

The old man smiled, "I see a lot of that kind."

"This one would have been here a month or so ago. My height, seventeen or eighteen years old, dark hair, duck tailed, black leather jacket. He was supposed to have picked up an antique car here. He should have been waiting for some time. Do you remember him?" Bart sat in a vacant chair. Alan looked around the store.

"That describes a lot of the young fellars now days." The old man stroked his chin thoughtfully, "Wait a minute. I did have a kid fitting that description. He bought a beer. The ID he gave me said he was older than I thought he looked." The old man looked at Bart quickly, "I always ID anyone who buys beer and his ID said he was old enough."

Bart chuckled and Alan frowned. Alan wanted information and Bart was getting too comfortable sitting there. "That is not why we're here. Beer sales are not our biliwhack. Now, tell me all you can remember about this kid." Bart smiled at Alan and shook his head no. He thought, if you get this old man shook up he won't be able to remember anything.

"He came in,, got a beer out of the box, and opened it before he came to the counter to pay for it. This irked me because I had not seen his ID yet. I looked at his ID and told him, "You're going to have pay for that beer and drink it outside."

"I'm going to drink in here out of the sun," the young man informed me.

"No, you're not!" I told him. "Federal law says you can't drink that beer on these premises. I'm not about to lose my license by letting you drink that beer in here."

"The punk took a long drink from the can and said, 'You know Pop, this beer tastes funny. I'm not going to pay for it.' I told him he paid for it and left the store or I'd sic the Sheriff on him. He paid for the beer and walked out the door. He stood in front of the door and drank that beer. I think his ID was fake. I think that is the reason he left. He didn't want the Sheriff looking at it."

"Did he drive the antique Model T off?" Alan held his breath.

"Nope, another leather jacketed punk picked him up on a motorcycle." The old man finished.

Bart heard the air gush out of Alan like he'd been hit in the belly with a fist. Alan's steps rang loudly as he marched toward the door. Holding both hands even with his head he yelled, "Another dead end."

Bart thanked the store owner and left. When he came through screen door Alan was standing with his hands on his hips looking down the road. Bart walked to the car's left door, tossed his briefcase into back seat and crawled behind the steering wheel.

Alan never said a word. He climbed into the passenger's seat and slammed the door extra hard when he closed it.

"We must talk." Bart was driving half as fast as Alan wanted to go.

"No, I'm not ready to throw in the Towel." Alan's jaw set.

"We're beginning to look like bigger fools by not being able to solve this case than that bootlegger could ever make us out be. I'm calling the director and asking him to bring the local directors around our area to a meeting. This operation has to be spread over a large section of the country and we haven't been able to figure where the whiskey is coming from or how it is being transported. I'm sure it not a local whiskey still.

"Humph," Alan growled and turned to the window. Although he usually ran things because Bart was a very laid back person, Bart was the senior partner and what Bart said was law. He'd been Bart's partner long enough to know that Bart was bulldog stubborn when he made a decision about something.

CHAPTER 14

Jason watched the prisoners come and go. When they came and went through the door Jason strained to see the parole board seated behind the desk. Some prisoners were happy and smiling. Others were sad.

Jason squirmed in his chair and rubbed his hands together. His insides were in a boil. The sharp taste of acid filled his mouth. He just had to get parole this time around. The Hitler moustache prevented him getting parole last time. They lost interest when they decided there was no way they could provoke Jason into his old ways.

Calm down, he told himself. *Don't go in there*

running your mouth. Your little girl is going to need you. With the amount of effort the Revenuers were putting into it they were bound to catch her sooner or later. If I'm there I can claim the still or do something to clear her.

"Jason Marley!" the speaker in the wall blared. Jason was in such turmoil he couldn't move. "Jason Marley," the speaker insisted. Jason shuffled through the door.

A woman sat between two men. She was reading a paper on her desk. "Sit down Jason." She waved a hand toward the chair in front of her desk. "You were a holy terror when you came in here," the lady turned a page.

"Yes mam," Jason mumbled.

"You quit having solitary and other punishments during a very short time period. Why?" The woman stared at Jason, judging his reply.

"Well ..., Jason weighed the question, "I came to realize my life was going no where. If I served my time and went out the chances were good that I'd be back. I don't want to come back after I leave here. I came to realize that I must get control of my temper and change my life style. I took anger management classes and it has been hard, Jason thought of the Hitler moustache, real hard, but I'm not the man I used to be."

"Could you help other prisoners come to this conclusion?" The lady asked.

Oh no, Jason thought. *I'm not going to stay here and work with other prisoners. What can I say to get out of this?* He sat silent looking at his hands.

"Jason?" the lady grew impatient.

"Sorry mam. I was weighing your question. I was looking back into my decision to change my life. It was a very personal decision. It was a very hard decision. I don't think anyone could have had much effect on me. I'm sure if anyone had tried to talk to me before I made the decision it would have been detrimental to both of us. It would have made me less likely to change and I'd probably have blown my top at them.

"I'm sorry, the answer is no I don't think I could have any luck with the other prisoners." Jason fell silent.

"Well." the lady picked up the loose sheets of paper and tapped them even on the desk, looked at the men sitting on either side of her and said, "Mr. Marley, we're going to grant your request for parole. It will take thirty to sixty days to process the paperwork. You will be reporting to a parole officer in your home county. He will place you in a halfway house for a period of time. Please don't do anything to make us sorry for paroling you."

It hit Jason like a thunderbolt. The tension gushed out of him, taking all his strength with it. "Th-Thank you," Jason stuttered. He tried to rise but it took a second effort to stand on his feet. Even then he needed a steadying hand on the desk.

He was going home! He could go keep the Revenuers' hands off his little girl.

"No Revenuer is going to send my little girl to a place like this," he growled to himself. It was a promise he intended to keep.

The drive to Penwick was long and tedious. Vera Lee's mind was in a swirl. How much had Clio told the Revenue Agents? Were they on her trail at this moment? Should she marry Billy Jack? Why was mother so adamant about staying in that house? What could she do about that? The possibilities, uncertainties and unknowns ate at her.

Billy Jack was waiting in the parking of the restaurant when she arrived.

The dinner was delicious. Vera Lee had not realized how hungry she was. She leaned back and watched the waiter whisk away the remaining scraps of the dinner along with the dirty dishes. The drive up had been tiring and Vera Lee was mentally exhausted from wrestling with problems. She needed this quiet relaxing evening to regroup her thoughts.

Wearing his cynical little grin Billy Jack had been quietly thoughtful all evening, giving Vera Lee room to gather sort and collect her thoughts. "Well, have you given any thought to the proposal?" Billy Jack spun the empty wine glass between his finger and thumb struggling to act nonchalant.

Vera Lee wiped her lips and folded the napkin very carefully and placed it on the table in front of her. "Yes," Vera Lee hesitated, "I have and I'm going to accept." Billy Jack started to jump up. Vera lee held a hand up to stop him. "There are some problems we must discuss. Mother must live with us until father gets out of prison. Mother informed me there was no way she was going to move out of that house in the valley. We will have to postpone the wedding until we work this out. I know you must stay here and work."

"Lets shut the whiskey still down and get married right away. I'll talk your mom into moving up here with us." Billy Jack was impatient.

"Poo, keep your shirt on," Vera Lee waved a hand. "I need five more loads and then we will shut the still down. I want a big wedding. I want the entire valley present when I say I do. That will take time to plan and do. In the mean time you can work on mom."

"We could make it without the next five loads of moonshine. The sawmill has never had a mortgage on it. I could borrow the same amount five loads would bring." Billy Jack searched for a way to speed things up."

"Then we'd be scrambling to pay it off." Vera Lee reached across the table and took his hand. Please be patient. Things are going along very well. If we get impatient we'll dump the apple cart. It won't be long. I do want you to look for a piece of land on the outskirts of town. I want to move into a new house when we get married."

"I'll take a couple days off and go home with you. We'll make this engagement official. We'll get your mom and run up to the prison to see Mr. Marley and make it right with him." Billy Jack began to plan and smiled at Vera Lee. "We could go up tonight."

The Pickup splashed water back onto the windshield when it crossed the creek in front of the house.

"You're supposed to slow down for that creek crossing," Vera Lee admonished.

"I don't feel like slowing down for anything. I feel like jumping in the air and telling the world I'm engaged to the world's prettiest girl." Billy Jack stopped in a cloud of dust at the yard gate.

"Do boys ever grow up?" Vera Lee asked Billy Jack while smiling and futilely trying to fan the dust away from her face.

"I hope not," Billy Jack said. "Why would a boy want grow up and spoil all the fun he's having."

A shadow rose from the porch swing and, moving into the glaring lights of the pickup and then leaned on a porch post.

Vera Lee was transfixed. She couldn't believe her eyes. "Daddy!" she screamed. Crying for joy she raced up the walk with both arms held up in front of her. Jason met her with open arms.

"What are you doing here? Did you escape? When did you get here?" Vera Lee was full of questions.

"Hold up for a minute!" Jason demanded. "I didn't escape. I got a parole. I got a twenty-four hour pass to come see the family and then I must report to a halfway house in the city. I was beginning to think I was going to miss you."

"We didn't know. Why didn't you tell us? We would have …," Vera Lee was confused.

"I didn't tell you because I didn't know if I was

going to get the parole or not. After I was granted Parole things went faster than I thought possible. I was out the next day" Jason explained.

Billy Jack shook hands with Jason, "We have a bit of news ourselves." He announced.

Ruth moved out of the shadows and took Jason by the arm, "Come in the house. I have a pot of coffee made." She said pulling on Jason's arm.

The moon was settling behind a low cloud. The day birds were beginning to chirp restlessly, eager for the growing light in the east to brighten into daylight. A rooster crowed and then two more confirmed his prediction of the coming daylight.

The group seated themselves around the table. Vera Lee stood behind Jason's chair with her hands on his shoulders. She was having a hard time convincing herself he was really here. Vera Lee looked at her mom. Ruth's face was glowing and her eyes had a fire in them Vera Lee had not seen since Jason went to prison. The coffee was hot and good.

"We have a bit of news," Bill Jack couldn't hold it

any longer, "I asked Vera Lee to be my wife and she has accepted. We came to ask for your blessing."

Jason hesitated. His plans had not included a son-in-law, "Can this wait until another time? I only have a few more minutes and then I must report to the halfway house. I want to feast my eyes on my wife and daughter. I don't have time to think about something that is going to affect us for a lifetime."

Billy Jack looked at Vera Lee and caught the imperceptible shake of her head.

Vera Lee would not have been so happy had she known the Revenoor's noose was tightening.

"I'm glad it is there instead of here," Chester hitched around to a more comfortable position in the chair. His waist line had considerably increased and the hair disappeared from the top of is head during the past years of relative peace.

"This is the problem," Dave stated. "We have a ring peddling moonshine whiskey north of us. They've been able to catch a few of the people selling the booze but no one, not even the people selling it, knows where it is being made. They've found no rot gut so they thought it all came from the same still.

They've found some bootleg whiskey in recent times that has a different chemical make up. The sale to the bootleggers was handled in a different manner. There is the possibility of having two different whiskey stills operating." Dave sat thoughtfully. He was weighing the possibilities as he went.

"There is the possibility that it is one whiskey still that is being moved around like Pots and the Swann brothers did years ago. If so, it is probably being moved from state to state. The different waters and possibly different supplies used to make the whiskey would account for the difference in the chemical makeup. It is all a high quality whiskey. They have found no rot gut so they think it all comes from the same still. "

"One thing I want you to remember is that this bootlegger is a wily coyote. Several times he has made Alan and Bart the laughing stock of the department. You guys proceed slowly and don't let that happen to us." Dave laid a sheaf of papers on the desk beside Harold.

"Yeah, we get a chuckle at that Alan. He about has a heart attack every time they get their hands on another bootlegger. We have been trying to decide which story was the best, the Priest and Nuns or the dog." Harold picked up the papers. Strong fingers quickly sorted the papers as he scanned them. He was the opposite of Chester. He had lost the weight Chester found. The hours he spent in the gym kept his shoulders where they belonged. "It must be a big whiskey still to produce enough shine to cover such a large area." He scratched his head.

Chester took the papers. He read them. Shaking his head he handed them back to Dave, "I haven't heard a thing. Not a ripple. I don't believe there is a whiskey still capable of running that much booze operating in our district."

"There seems to be no ripple anywhere but the bootleggers are being supplied by someone. The Director has called for a meeting of the District Directors in Wichita, KS. We are on the edge of this area so I've been ordered to attend.

"I want to be prepared when I get there. You guys call in your stoolies and talk to them. Chester you check the sugar consumption and supply end of it. See if you find anyone selling or buying more sugar than they should be.

"There are two new sugar refineries in Louisiana. Go, don't call, you will learn more that way. Check all their sales records. Check with all the warehouse distribution points," Dave stopped to catch his breath.

Chester shifted in his seat, "An agent named Bart called from Nebraska and wanted me to check this sugar deal out sometime back. The only thing I could find in the way of an unusual increase in the use of sugar was a small bakery in Keene, Texas. It recently changed hands. The new owner put a young lady, who worked there, in charge of the place. The new manager is a go getter. The business is growing by leaps and bounds.

"I went by the bakery and decided the rapid growth of the business accounted for the increased use of sugar. .

"The new sugar refineries have caused a lot of the farmers to plant sugar cane. The refineries don't use the sorghum by product from the sugar refining process. They sell it to feed companies. The feed companies mix it with their livestock feed.

"Some farmers make sorghum and sell it alongside the highway. A gallon of sorghum will make more alcohol than a gallon of sugar," Chester rambled on.

"Harold, will you check with the Highway Patrol. Give them pictures of the latest whiskey transporting cars we have caught and alert them to the possibility of bootleg whiskey being transported north out of our district. I will take care of notifying the County Sheriff's Departments and City Police forces along the way." Dave was relieved to be doing something again.

On his way north Dave caught up with a loaded log truck. He was forced to follow for a couple of miles. *That is some good looking Red Oak logs*, he thought, *too bad we don't have sawmills near home to cut those logs into lumber and the factories to convert them into furniture.. It would supply some good jobs and make Moonshinning a less tempting proposition. I've heard they sell every scrap they haul. They chip everything that don't make lumber and sell it for landscaping. Oh well, the cutting and hauling furnishes some jobs in our area. God knows we need them.*

The road opened up into a short passing area with no on coming traffic. Dave slapped the accelerator to the floor. Zipping past the truck he was too preoccupied to look up and recognize Louis as the driver.

Mile after mile Dave pounded the pavement. All the while his mind was stirring all the facts of the case. He was looking for the missing link. There must be something everyone overlooked. He was exhausted when he wheeled the agency pickup into a parking lot in front of the building designated as the meeting place.

A swift prairie breeze ruffled his hair and rattled the paperwork in his hand as he hurried across the pavement before the door. Shortening his steps he pushed the door to the interior. The room had a damp smell to it.

All the Area Directors sat up front. Alan sat two Rows back to show his distain and belief it wasn't necessary. Dave took a seat in the row in front of Alan.

"We have gathered you here today because we have a problem …," the National Director droned into the microphone. The National Director read the significant parts of the case. Dave and the other directors took notes as they saw fit.

"As of now, no agents have been threatened with violence. We have had a suspect killed in a jail cell. As Bart and Alan can tell you. This is a crafty individual or group we are working with." The National director closed.

Dave felt Alan cringe when his name was mentioned. The group broke up into brainstorming segments. Years of experience kicked the problem around.

The brain storming sessions broke up when the sun, hanging low on the western horizon, began pushing fiery fingers of red and orange across the clouds. The prairie breeze had grown into a monster wind howling at the eves of the building.

Dave rushed to his pickup with a bent head. He fumbled hurriedly with the keys at the pickup door. Diving into the truck Dave let the wind blow the door shut, closing itself out of the truck.

Easing the truck down the right lane Dave read the signs until he found one that said RESTAURANT. The howling wind pushed and shoved Dave through the door. He was holding his paperwork and notes with both hands.

Seating himself in the back corner of the dining room he looked out the window. An empty fifty-five gallon oil drum come tumbling down the street. It went past the automobiles parked in the parking lot at a high rate of speed and disappeared past the next building.

"Enough is enough," Dave told himself, "I'm going to have a nice leisurely dinner, get a room and stay the night." He put in his order, took a sip of the hot coffee and took a table phone off the wall. He was dialing Chester to apprise him of the day's events and find what if anything Chester had learned.

The door opened and a man backed in holding the door against the raging wind. Billy Jack! Dave thought. He had not seen Billy Jack since the moonlight night he'd used the black car to run him down and arrested him for hauling a load of illegal whiskey.

Holding the phone and turning his head so it broke up his profile Dave studied the man out of the corner of his eye. It was Billy Jack!

CHAPTER 15

Good food covered the entire table. Even though it was broad daylight candles were set on both ends and in the middle of the table. Every piece of the old fine china was on the table. A few new pieces had been purchased to compliment it. The silver candle holders were polished to perfection. The reflections of the sunlight off the silverware beside each plate put dapple patterns on the walls and ceiling.

It was a meal fit for a king. It was Jason's welcome home dinner. It was the first time the family sat at the table together in many years. An extra plate was set. Billy Jack had been invited to the welcome home celebration.

Ruth buzzed in from the kitchen with the last bowl of food and took her place at the foot of the table. Her hair was put up in the style she had worn at her wedding so many years ago. She was dressed in her finest. She glowed with a fire and health Vera Lee had not seen since Jason went to prison.

Vera Lee studied her Dad. He'd aged considerably. The scars on his face and hands bore witness to the battles with other prisoners and the brutal Hitler mustache guard group. His demeanor was quieter than she remembered. He seemed to think before he spoke. His eyes missed nothing. Like a hunted animal he was constantly alert.

In a way his prison battles had served him well. The hours of weight lifting, calisthenics and isometric exercises he did to keep himself in shape to fight those battles kept his body in good order and healthy. The only down side was he'd learned that at times he had to make quick decisions and act on them instantly without time for thought.

Yes, Jason was a changed man. He was the man

who left here whipped and chiseled to a fine point.

Jason watched his little girl out of the corner of his eye. She had grown into a beautiful woman. She wasn't his little girl anymore. There none of the shrinking violet left in her. The hard lines around her eyes and mouth were not there when he left. She had grown into a tough no nonsense business woman.

Jason glanced across the table at Billy Jack and wondered if he'd done the right thing in fighting so hard to keep her from marrying Dave Maloy. If she had married Dave she would be living in a cozy house and still be his little girl. She wouldn't have had to face the hard facts of life that brought out the Marley blood in her.

Jason's chest swelled with pride. The Marley blood still ran true and dang it, Dave Maloy was still a turncoat. He was a sorry son of the valley who turned on his own people.

Yep he had made the right decision in fighting to keep Vera Lee from marrying that piece of trash. *Heck,* he thought," *My grandchildren would have been half Revenuers."*

Jason stared out the window. He still couldn't believe he was free to walk out and enjoy the cool breeze, listen to the birds chirp; the insects buzz, and enjoy the sight of the lush green countryside.

Billy Jack was beginning to feel like the forgotten man. He was definitely the outsider here. Perhaps he shouldn't have come. What was Jason's return going to do to their up coming wedding? What was it going to do to his and Vera Lee's life together after the wedding?

When Billy Jack first learned of Jason's return he was elated. Jason would be there to care for Ruth. He and Vera Lee would be free to marry and move on.

Now it appeared there was a new bull of the woods on the scene intending to take over. Vera was pandering to Jason's every wish. The Vera Lee Billy Jack knew was a tough, independent woman. He had never seen this Vera Lee before.

Billy Jack maintained a silence as long as he could stand it. "What do you think of our up coming wedding?" he asked Jason.

A fork full of food stopped halfway to Jason's mouth. His gray eyes speared Billy Jack like twin light beams. "Later!" he growled. The eyes flicked briefly to Ruth and then returned to Vera Lee. The fork finished its journey. Jason chewed thoughtfully. *I'm gonna lose this one. I'm going to loose,* he thought, *because I have both women against me. The only way I could win was shoot him without warning.*

Looking at Billy Jack again he softened his stance with, "We'll discuss it after supper. I haven't had food or company like this in a long time and I want to enjoy it."

The regal meal melted down into empty bones and dirty plates. Dessert had followed the meal. With the dessert finished everyone was leaning back, sated and comfortable.

Ruth rose and began stacking her dessert plate onto the dirty plate. "You all go out on the porch and discuss Vera Lee's and Billy Jack's wedding. I'll do the dishes."

"Leave the dishes and I will do them." Vera Lee

protested.

"There ain't no butterfingered child going to wash and chip my fine china." Ruth began waving her hands in motion like she was chasing flies and shouting,"Shoo, shoo,"

Chairs rattled and clanked while the group settled down on the porch. Each had settled in such a manner as to be facing one another. Vera Lee moved her chair so as to be a little closer to Billy Jack.

"All right Billy Jack," Jason opened the conversation. "A few years ago I'd have kicked your seat from here to the highway and back if I'd thought you had such a notion as to marry my little girl. I'd made up my mind that she was not going to marry any of this whiskey crowd. I wanted her to marry someone who could and would do right for her.

"Ruth and Vera Lee have told me about your success as a business man. They have about convinced me you might be the man. I'm telling you now, and I'm telling you plain, if you ain't this man I'll be after her and bring her home.

"I'll take over the whiskey still now. You two get married move out of here as soon as possible."

This sounded good to Billy Jack but Vera Lee flew out her chair yelling, "NO! Daddy you cannot go near a still! You must not even take a drink until your probation is finished. They will send you back to prison for that." The business woman was back. Hands on her hips, feet spread and head tilted Vera Lee pointed a finger at Jason. "We're going to run five more loads and then shut the still down for good. Our businesses are doing fine. We will have enough to live comfortably and perhaps help you and mom if you need it."

'We sure won't need help if I run the still. I know how. I did it for years until that sneaky Dave Maloy came back into the picture." Jason puffed up

"The still is shut down right now. We're going to sit on this porch for a week to celebrate and catch up on things. After that we're going to run five more loads and I'm going to take an ax to the stills myself!" Vera Lee became more adamant. "You are not going to leave mom and me again! Understood! You're going to stay away from moonshine and anyone making or drinking it!"

Jason settled back. His mouth worked but no words came out. The sixth sense he developed in prison warned him to get out of this, for now at least.

"Jeff and Junior Rayette, are working for me now. They will stay and help you work the place. Farm goods and livestock prices have come up. I think you can make a living off the place.

"The hog house is making a ton of money right now. If you don't make enough I'll hire you as CEO and Mister Harper can train you. You listen to me," Vera Lee bent over with her nose almost touching his like she used to when she was a little girl. "Do not go anywhere near a whiskey still!"

Jason laughed. "Go get married. I'll be a good boy until I lend you to this lummox." Leaning his head he looked at Billy Jack, "You better be good," he warned.

CHAPTER 16

Billy Jack backed into the restaurant and secured the door against the wind. Apparently he failed to recognize Dave when his glance swept the patrons already seated. Turning he waved at the waitress and seated himself at the first booth. He sat with his back to Dave. Dave's eyes measured the width of the shoulders. Billy Jack had grown into a big man and gained a lot weight.

From Billy Jack's familiarity with the waitress Dave figured he must eat here often. Slick shave, well groomed hair, nice suit, beautiful shirt, matching tie and shiny shoes. Dave had trouble connecting this evidently successful businessman with the wild cowboy booted kid wearing the big hat he'd put the handcuffs on that faithful night years ago.

Dave got his meal and ate slowly. With Billy Jack seated close to the door many people walked past his table. All nodded or spoke. Some of the customers stopped and passed small conversation.

"Evidently he eats here often and lives near by. He seems to know everyone and is well liked." Dave talked to himself. A sixth sense kept him from shaking hands with Billy Jack. Billy Jack might not want to shake hands with the man who sent him to prison.

It looks like he ought to thank me, Dave thought, *He never would have been as successful running whiskey as he apperars to be now.*

Billy Jack ate his supper and left without recognizing Dave. The wind was dying down. Dave paid his bill and set out to find a motel. He would get good nights sleep and meet Harold and Chester at the office to see what kind of luck they were having.

When he turned into the parking lot at the office the next day Dave smiled. Chester's car was parked in the parking spot Labeled DIRECTOR. It happened regularly. Dave wondered if it was still a joke or if Chester was saying he should have been promoted instead of Dave.

"The wandering Jew returns," Harold said when Dave pushed the door open. He was seated at the end of Dave's desk sorting papers.

"What greetings do you have for us from the great White Father?" Chester was seated in Dave's chair behind the desk.

"He said for you to get out of my chair and to never sit there again. He said I was going to skin you the next time you readjusted my chair." Dave was smiling but he was half serious.

"How did you guys make out? Did you come with anything while I was gone?"

"We have a ripple. The manager of a sorghum warehouse called me. A truck comes in occasionally and picks up a load of sorghum. He's been in several times. The truck doesn't have any writing or company name on the door. The manager said they'd had no reason to get the tag number. It could be a rancher who uses the sorghum to manufacture livestock feed but we need to look into it. I was thinking of sending one of the young agents to stake the place out and follow the truck. I'd tell him not do anything to give himself away. Just gather information. Then I decided to wait for you. How do you want us to handle it?"

Dave was silently thoughtful for a time. "Bart was telling me about this bootlegger. He is a wile coyote. He has Alan so tied up in knots he didn't talk to us at the meeting. He sat off behind the group.

I'm going to send you down there. I want someone with experience and common sense on this investigation. We will keep it between the three of us.

"You're right. Keep this to an information gathering trip even if that truck happens lead you to a whiskey still. We want the transport people and whoever is selling the stuff.

"I also want you to take that grinning fat man sitting over there with you. Perhaps that will keep him out of my parking place and from behind my desk." Dave pointed a finger.

"Here's our report on the investigation so far. There is nothing remarkable. It keeps a record of our activities. More fodder for the filing cabinet." Harold passed the paper work he'd been thumbing through to Dave.

"You guy get back to me now. I have another meeting with the District Directors next week. The Director wants all the District Directors to get together and compare notes. I'll need anything you have found brought to me no later than Thursday morning.

After Harold and Chester left Dave diligently read the report turned in by his agents. He noted the sugar use by the bakery in Keene, Texas had actually declined. Chester'd made a note of the bakery being relocated into a large grocery store and the bakery's manager now managed both the grocery and the bakery. She may have become too busy to push the bakery as hard as she had in the past.

Dave leaned back to think. A vision of Billy Jack

floated before his eyes. Billy Jack was Dave's idea of what a successful business man should look like. Dave knew Billy Jack was smart, resourceful, and a hard worker but had thought him too wild and reckless to manage a business or do anything requiring steady judgment and perseverance. His time in prison must have slowed him down and steadied him up.

In the past Dave had spent many days and nights trying to catch Billy Jack. It wasn't until he'd built the black car that he could match Billy Jack's speed on the highway and skill on the back roads.

It had been a long and hard race. Billy Jack made the first and final mistake that fateful night.

Rocking forward in his chair Dave pulled himself back into the present reality. I wonder where he got the money to start with, Dave mused, and one of these days I'm going to ask him. It would be nice to get some of these other boys in the valley set up. It would lessen the temptation to make whiskey.

The phone rang thee times and Robin answered.

"Robin this is Vera Lee."

"I was just thinking about you. I heard that civilization had reached your part of the world. I was going to try to find your new telephone number and see if I could get through." Robin sounded cheerful.

"I have some news. Billy Jack asked me to marry him and I accepted. We're going to get married." Vera Lee was trying to remain calm but the excitement was building in her.

"Eeeeyeah," Robin squealed. "Congratulations, I have been hoping. He is really a nice guy. I have known him a long time."

A pang of jealousy shot through Vera Lee. "How long have you known Billy Jack?"

"When I was a kid Billy Jack Ran a load of moonshine for Dad, I believe I was about ten and boy did I have a crush on him. Billy Jack was just a teenager then." Robin said. "My big problem was that he treated me like I was a little kid. When is this wedding going to happen?"

"We've set no date yet," the pang of jealousy was wearing off.

"I have news also. J. D. asked me to marry him and I said yes." Robin gushed. "That is why I was trying to get your number."

"And when is this to take place?" Vera Lee thought it funny that she had no feeling about J.D. marrying someone.

"We've set no date as of now. We are both so busy." Robin was silent for a moment. "Are you and Billy Jack going to live in the valley?"

"No, I'm going to Nebraska with Billy Jack." Vera Lee recovered from her pang of jealousy

"What is this going to mean for our partnership and the store?" Robin asked.

"Well, I'm not sure. I have considered it and planned to go on pretty much like we have been in the past but now that I find you're getting married also I don't know what your plans are. Are you going to stay on as Manager or are you going to quit and be a housewife? What are your plans?" Vera Lee was getting worried.

"J.D. and I have discussed it. I could never be a stay at home housewife. I'm so busy and he has such a large case load we're going to defer our honeymoon until a later date and continue on pretty much as usual." Robin said.

"I'll tell you what, why don't we think this thing out. I'll call you later. You discuss it with J.D. I'll talk it over with Billy Jack and we can make firm plans. I hate to have loose ends hanging." Vera Lee hung up and sat drumming her fingers on the table top.

Elis Holder's eyes were going back and forth like windshield wipers. He was as nervous as a cat on a hot tin roof. He'd picked up his first load of moonshine whiskey.

His buddy, Tim Thadworth, had picked up a load and was now bragging about how much money he made selling it.

"It's a new still opened up in Southeast Oklahoma. The fellow came up here with a load. He's coming back. You should join me. I ain't ever made this much money this easy and this fast." Tim was enthusiastic.

Having lost his job and being out of work for several months had drawn Elis's saving account to almost zero.

Elis decided to try bootlegging. Tim introduced Elis to his middleman. The middleman agreed to supply Elis. It had taken all the meager savings he could muster to purchase this load. Tim assured him he could sell it and triple his money in less than a week. He decided to try.

The farther he went the more nervous he became. He was sure everyone was looking through the metal at the cases of jars in the trunk of his car or through the doors at the two cases that would not fit into the trunk.

What is that up there beside the road? Oh no, it is a highway patrol car! He knew it was going to happen he just knew it. He was so nervous he his hands were shaking on the steering wheel.

Elis zipped past the patrol car with one eye glued to the rear view mirror. Officer Jordan glanced at the tag and then back at the driver. He could see the driver glued to the rearview mirror watching him.

Grunting in satisfaction officer Jordan flipped the switches and gunned the engine. The lights on top of the patrol began rotating. With red reflections bouncing off highline poles, fences, cars and anything else nearby the patrol car shot onto the highway behind Elis. Looking at his speedometer Elis's heart almost stopped. Seventy miles per hour on a sixty mile per hour road! How could he have messed up this bad?

Hold on, he told himself. Take your ticket and go.

"Driver's license and registration please," The Patrolman was business like.

Elis fumbled and was slow to get the billfold out of his hip pocket. The patrolman was not slow about noticing the boxes on the back seat. Each box had the company logo on them and MASON JARS written across the side in bold black letters. This fit neatly into the alert the Revenue Agents had spread.

"I stopped you because you were going seventy in a sixty mile per hour speed limit and you never slowed for the red-light. Please step out of the car."

Later, Alan and Bart had been hammering on Elis for three hours. He was so nervous he was shaking like he was freezing. He passed no information. He was too scared to talk.

Bart rubbed his stomach, "I'm hungry, let's go eat lunch. We got this fellow nailed anyway," he stared at Elis. "We don't even have to work at it. We're already got enough to get him twenty years in the hoosegow." Bart gave Alan a knowing look. Alan swelled up but followed Bart out of the interrogation room.

"I almost had him broke!" Alan protested when the door closed behind him.

"You had him so scared he was unable to think or talk. He was near a heart attack. That is just what we need. Another dead witness. Remember we've lost two witnesses. Give him some time to calm down and think about the twenty years I mentioned and he will sing like a canary when we offer him a way out." Bart turned to the uniformed officer doing guard duty, "Give him his cigarettes, a paper cup of water and a cup of coffee."

Alan groaned in disgust and tromped away.

An hour later Bart and Alan entered the interrogation room. Bart noticed with satisfaction the ash tray had several cigarette butts in it, the water and coffee cups were dry. Bart waved Alan to the end of the table. This meant remain quiet and let me handle it for now.

"I'm sorry we have to bother you like this Elis but we have forms and stuff that have to be filled out to process you in. We don't need anymore information to get you twenty years. Of course you could cut many of those years off if you helped yourself. You could perhaps get it down to five year probation if you give us the right information."

"What do I have to do to get it down to five years probation?"

"You have to tell us all you know. If you give us the right information we'll talk to the judge." Bart explained.

"Not good enough. I admit I'm scared to death. Twenty years I'd never survive but if I spill my guts you might not figure it was good enough because you have what I know. I want five years probation guaranteed before I talk."

"Let us confer. We might go for this if you tell us

what we want to know. If we go for it and you don't come through truthfully, we'll pin another charge on you and send you to the worst hellhole we can find." Bart nodded to Alan and walked through the door.

"What is the deal offering him that much immunity this early," Alan demanded when they reached their desks.

"Aw, don't worry he's going to split like an over ripe watermelon. Besides, I ran a make on him through the National Program. Can you believe this guy has a totally clean record? There's not even a traffic ticket on it. None of these bleeding heart judges will give him over five years probation anyway." Bart said rising.

"Ok," Bart settled in with paper and pen. We're going to give you immunity, no more than five years suspended if you spill all. How did you get into this?"

"Well, I need money real bad. I've been out of work for sometime. A friend set me up to meet a fellow …"

Bart's hand flew up, "WHO set you up to meet

this fellow?"

Elis hesitated.

"It's all or nothing," Bart growled.

"Ok," Elis surrendered, "Tim Tadworth"

"And where do we find this Tim?' Bart was writing vigorously.

"Next door to my house," Elis was feeling awful.

"Who delivered the whiskey to you," Bart stopped and looked up. This was a crucial question.

"I don't know."

"Remember it's all or nothing," Bart rested both elbows on the table, twisting the pencil between his hands.

Alan sat at attention at the end of the table.

"I really don't know. He parked the pickup in a side road near the highway and we carried the cases to the car," Elis rubbed his eyes trying to remember.

"What state was the license plate issued in?" Bart asked softly and held his breath.

"There were no license plates on the pickup." Elis was sweating he knew he was not providing the info they wanted.

"Did you see both the front and back of the pickup."

Alan slumped at the end of the table. Another dead end.

"Wait, he backed the pickup off the road, we had to carry the whiskey past the front each time. I remember glancing through the window and seeing a letter lying on the seat. It was addressed to Jim Hart. The reason I remember is my wife's maiden name was Hart."

Alan's head snapped up and he was listening again.

"What was the address on the letter?" Bart was scribbling.

"I don't know. This was a tough looking man with a pistol strapped on his side, I just wanted to get out of there," Elis waved a finger.

"What kind of truck?" Bart kept up the rapid fire questions. He wanted to keep Elis off balance.

"It was Ford about ten years old. It was green, a faded green."

"What did this man look like? Give me a

description." Bart demanded.

Elis was silent for awhile. "Big man, lots of muscle, a pistol strapped on the outside, thin blond hair." Elis really remembered the pistol.

"How tall was he and how much do you think he weighed?" Bart questioned.

"About six feet two inches tall and I'd guess about two-hundred and twenty pounds."

Bart and Alan questioned Elis for several more hours but never got anymore significant information from him.

Back at their desks Alan and Bart went over the results of the information from Elis' questioning.

"It doesn't sound right. The method of operation does not fit our wily coyote man. These people did stupid stuff I don't think our man would do." Bart said.

"Unless he's setting us up again. He has me leery. He may have some kind of plan, some kind of trap waiting for us. This man has made us look real bad. I want him! We're going to have move slow and be careful. I don't want to be laughed at again." Alan's face turned red at the thought.

"What's the matter? Don't you feel a lot better after donating all that money to the widow's and orphans fund," Bart chuckled.

Alan's face turned even redder. "Now, all we have to do is go through the million names in the Department of Motor Vehicles looking for a Jim Hart who owns a green Ford pickup of an undetermined year." Alan was glum. "This could be what Wile E. is setting us up for."

"I think we should check the outstanding warrants first. From Elis's description this guy sounds kind of arrogant, with the gun on the outside in plain sight and all. He sounds like a bully who wants to impress people with his bad man stuff. I'll call all the District Directors offices and have them check their areas for this Jim Hart." Bart closed his notebook.

"You might wait on that call until we find out if we're being set up again." Alan said morosely.

Dave was loaded and ready to depart to the meeting when Harold and Chester burst into his office like a couple of school boys. "We've found the still!" They announced.

"It's on federal land on the Red River. We'll have to catch them operating it." Chester eased his bulk into a chair.

"It's a big still too. We followed the syrup truck to it. It would be possible for it to supply the area we are helping up north." Harold said.

"Keep a loose surveillance. We want all the operators and more importantly we want the transporters so we can tie it in with our agents up north. Put a raiding party together but let no one outside this room know we have found the still. Tell them it is a training exercise until we are ready to move." Dave was elated.

At the meeting Dave pulled Alan and Bart aside. Bart brought Dave up to the present on the Jim Hart affair.

"That is great! I have news for you two. We have found the still. It's …

"What?" Alan exclaimed.

"We found the still," Dave started again. "It's on Red River. We're prepared to raid it as soon as you can find this Jim Hart and we get a line on the transporters. I'd appreciate it if you boys kept this under your hats and told no one until we're ready to wrap it up." Dave finished.

When Dave finished with the meeting he decided to talk to Billy Jack. Perhaps he could get Billy Jack to speak to the young men graduating from Valley High. Billy Jack could give them pointers about how to enter the business world.

When Dave reached the sawmill it was shut down. The place was deserted except for a car parked at the office. Dave's Revenuer instincts kicked in and he parked the car behind a hedge down the street and settled back to observe.

After a long spell of peaceful observance Dave was chiding himself for being a suspicious person. He would go see if that car belonged to Billy Jack. He reached for the key. Before the engine started a loaded log truck came around the corner.

Dave settled back in the seat. The truck entered the mill and swung around in a circle. The door opened and Louis stepped out! Louis was older and much heavier but Dave would recognize him anywhere.

Billy Jack appeared driving a forklift. Louis removed the bindings holding the logs on the truck and Billy Jack removed one log from the load and took it into a lumber storage building. Louis followed and closed the door.

Dave waited a few minutes and took a chance. He walked through the gate and peeped through a crack into the building. Billy Jack and Louis were draining a liquid from the log into quart jars.

It was with a heavy heart Dave drove from the Sawmill to the court house. He asked the clerk to see a copy of the deed to the sawmill and the furniture factories. The clerk laid the books containing the documents on the counter.

Dave opened the first and thumbed to the appropriate page. He ran his finger down to the name of the registered owner. Ruth Stiller? Ruth Stiller? Why that was Vera Lee's mother's maiden name!

The full import of these facts hit him like a sledge

hammer. His knees nearly buckled. He was sick to his stomach. He thumbed up the other deeds and his consternation deepened.

The clerk rose from her desk and approached Dave, "Are you alright sir?" she queried.

Dave looked at her and dashed to the bathroom without a word.

On the way home he beat the steering wheel, yelled and screamed. He knew the full impact of the situation. Ruth would never do this thing. It was Vera Lee operating under Ruth's name. What could he do? What did he want to do? What, what??

Chester's mention of the bakery in Keene, Texas came to mind. He took the road to Keene. He staggered out of the courthouse. The bakery and the store were both in Ruth Stiller's name.

The bakery had been an early purchase. Of course it was to cover the sugar the still used to make whiskey. The store could also be used to cover sugar use. Chester said the bakery had used less sugar when he checked a few days ago.

Robin Kowlowsky was listed as part owner and

manager? The name kept bugging him. Then it hit him with full import. John Kowlowsky. Several years ago he arrested a still operator. Robin, the still operator's daughter, was a child then but she attacked Dave with both fists. She was pulled off by her Grandmother Whooten.

Dave shook his head at the memories of Granny Whooten. She was the old lady who blocked the road when he was chasing the elusive black Ford.

The car splashed water and squashed three minnows when he crossed the creek. Vera Lee and the Rayette brothers were walking from the barn when Dave screeched to a stop before the gate. Vera Lee was carrying an ax in her hand. The Rayette brothers gave him an angry look of hate and climbing into their truck drove off.

Vera Lee walked toward him.

"Vera Lee, put that ax down," Dave ordered sternly.

Vera Lee recognized how upset Dave was. She looked at the ax like it was the first time she had seen it. Tossing it aside she continued to approach

Dave. "Dave I ..." she began to say.

Jason leaned against the door and peeped around the facing. Dave and Vera Lee were too far away to understand the words but he could hear the angry tones and see the body language.

"Don't you even start to lie to me! Do you realize the extent of your actions?" He demanded. "You have set your mother up for a long stretch of time in prison. He held his hands up in front of him and began counting on his fingers; you, your mother, Jason, Robin, Billy Jack, Louis and the Rayette brothers are all looking at a long term in prison. That is the list so far. There will be others."

"Robin knew nothing of the still. Mother or Dad never went near the still." Vera Lee managed.

"Robin is implicated with covering for the sugar. She knew what was going on. Jason is here on the property with a whiskey still. I'm sure he knows it's here. That's a violation of his probation. Your mother's name is on the deeds for the businesses covering the still. It will go worse for her than any of the rest of you." Dave turned his back and slapped his hands together in agitation.

"Dave I ...," Vera Lee began.

"Shut up!" Dave ordered.

The Marley steel rose in Vera Lee. Her back straightened. Her hands came to rest on her hips. "I don't care what you say Mother, Father nor Robin had anything to do with the still. It was mine! I planned it! I built it! I operated it! There is no still anymore. I just destroyed it! We quit making whiskey!" Vera Lee's chin rose in defiance. "Billy Jack and I are getting married and I'm moving to Nebraska. Mom and Dad are going to stay here."

"You were too late destroying the still. We have enough evidence to convict you as it is. I'm sure one of your cohorts will turn states evidence and implicate you even farther.

"You will do what the court tells you to do. Billy Jack and Louis deserve another long prison sentence. The Rayette brothers need a firm lesson. You planned and ran the thing. I could see you go to prison. I feel sorry for Robin and Jason

"You've tied your mother in as the chief culprit

in this operation. You can't imagine what is going to happen to her when she falls into the tender clutches of Alan and Bart. Your man up north has made them look like idiots and they're burning for revenge.

"Ruth is a second mother to me. I know she is innocent. I cannot arrest her. I will not let one of my agents arrest her. You've finally achieved your objective of taking this star off my chest!" Dave walked a circle slapping his fist into his open palm.

"Dave I ..." Vera started again

"Now, you shut up and stand there and hear me out! And you listen good!" Dave pointed a finger at her. So far I'm the only one who knows of your involvement in the whiskey business.

"We have found a big still operating south of here. I'm going to feed those poor bastards to Alan and Bart. I'll do my best to divert all attention to the still we're busting. You get rid of all the evidence of a whiskey still here. You call Billy Jack and tell him to dump every drop of whiskey he has on hand and destroy the hollow logs.

"And Vera Lee, if one more drop of whiskey goes north I will see you rot in prison. Ruth is the only reason I'm putting my career and occupation in jeopardy. This could cost me my badge very easily. I want you to take these handcuffs and hang them on your wall. If you think about getting cute you look at them and think about what it will be like wearing them." Dave took the handcuffs and extended them to Vera Lee hanging from his fingertips.

"Oh no you don't!" Jason said aloud, "No one is going to arrest my little girl!" Taking the rifle from the pegs above the door he checked the load and leaned the barrel against the door facing. When the sights settled on the space between Dave's shoulder blades he pulled the trigger.

It had been years since Jason fired a rifle. The bullet hit a little high and to the left of where he intended.

The impact spun Dave to the ground. He instinctively drew his service weapon as he went down. Jason came charging across the porch. Dave rose to a sitting position. Jason stopped and raised the rifle.

"No!" Vera Lee screamed and leaped between Dave and her father. The big bullet hit her with a sickening thump and she rolled into the dirt beside Dave.

Dave's eyesight was failing fast. He thumbed a shot at Jason and slowly rolled to his side. His head came to rest on Vera Lee.

The bullet hit Jason in the breast bone and took a cupful of his backbone out the backside.

Ruth came out of the kitchen to see what all the shooting was about. She came through the door wiping her hands on her apron. Her legs carried her across the porch before her eyes could convince her brain they weren't lying to it. Her mouth dropped open and her hand rose to her chest. Her knees buckled and she tumbled into the rose bushes at the edge of the porch

The great owl, disturbed by the gun fire, hooted a question to his mate. The sound rolled on, unheard by the deaf ears in the yard.

Other Books written by Erman Sands:

Shad

Spirit of the Wolf

Battle of Whiskey Valley

Made in the USA
Lexington, KY
13 September 2018